Pastoral Care in Schools

This is the ultimate guide to pastoral care, offering practical advice, guidance and resources for all, whether you are starting out on your journey into pastoral care or are an experienced school leader.

The book brings together the different roles and responsibilities that pastoral staff have in schools, including teacher, mentor, social worker, counsellor, careers advisor, referee and much more. It offers no-nonsense guidance and strategies for pastoral staff at all levels that can be implemented immediately. Chapters cover key topics such as:

- Finding the right pastoral role; applications and interviews
- Behaviour management
- Attendance
- Safeguarding
- Leading staff and students
- Working with parents

Full of case studies and examples of real practice, this guide is essential reading for all aspiring and experienced pastoral staff at all levels that want to make a real difference to their school culture and shape how it cares for and supports its pupils.

Connor Acton is Deputy Headteacher in a Multi-Academy Trust in the East Midlands and Chair of an Academy Board of Trustees.

Pastoral Care in Schools

Developing Yourself, Your School and Your Community

Connor Acton

LONDON AND NEW YORK

Designed cover image: © Getty Images

First published 2026
by Routledge
4 Park Square, Milton Park, Abingdon, Oxon OX14 4RN

and by Routledge
605 Third Avenue, New York, NY 10158

Routledge is an imprint of the Taylor & Francis Group, an informa business

© 2026 Connor Acton

The right of Connor Acton to be identified as author of this work has been asserted in accordance with sections 77 and 78 of the Copyright, Designs and Patents Act 1988.

All rights reserved. No part of this book may be reprinted or reproduced or utilised in any form or by any electronic, mechanical, or other means, now known or hereafter invented, including photocopying and recording, or in any information storage or retrieval system, without permission in writing from the publishers.

Trademark notice: Product or corporate names may be trademarks or registered trademarks, and are used only for identification and explanation without intent to infringe.

British Library Cataloguing-in-Publication Data
A catalogue record for this book is available from the British Library

ISBN: 978-0-367-74305-5 (hbk)
ISBN: 978-0-367-74307-9 (pbk)
ISBN: 978-1-003-15704-5 (ebk)

DOI: 10.4324/9781003157045

Typeset in Melior
by SPi Technologies India Pvt Ltd (Straive)

Contents

	Introduction	1
1	Pastoral Care in Schools (Systems/Roles)	3
2	Vision and Values in Pastoral Care	10
3	Developing Pastoral Care Experience	24
4	Finding/Securing Pastoral Care Roles	35
5	Leading Staff	51
6	Behaviour Management	67
7	Attendance/Punctuality	88
8	Administration	99
9	Safeguarding	107
10	Working with Parents and Carers	118
11	Pastoral Care and the Curriculum	132
	Conclusion	142
	Index	144

Introduction

You never quite know where the world of Pastoral Care will take you, but one thing is for sure – there's nothing else quite like it! This book reflects on my experience in Pastoral Care in a multitude of roles, across a number of schools and offers practical advice and guidance based on this experience. I have been privileged to hold varied positions that have allowed me to develop experience across many disciplines and, above all else, work with and support children from all walks of life.

If you are reading this book, it's likely that you have some form of interest or connection to pastoral care. I hope that it will be a number of things; a starting point for those of you who are new to the world of pastoral care; a refresher, or a friendly walk through familiar territory, for those of you who are veterans of our ever-developing field and a useful, practical guide with tips and tricks designed with the express purpose of translating into immediate action.

Pastoral Care is not what it was ten, five or even two years ago at the time that I write this. The world we live in is one fraught with difficulty for the students in our care and there are more barriers for them to overcome than ever before. It follows, then, that there continues to be an ever-evolving set of issues and problems for us to solve with, and for, them. My hope is that this book, whatever your role or experience is, will provide some useful advice, anecdotes and ideas that will stand the test time of time as we traverse this complicated environment. I have also sought to provide a multitude of opportunities for reflection throughout because, in Pastoral Care, half of the game is asking questions of ourselves and others and learning from what has been done in the past!

I attempt to cover many facets of Pastoral Care through both the eyes of individuals and educational establishments. Each chapter is dedicated to one of these areas and many are supported by the kind sharing of information from school staff across the UK to illustrate points and provide real-world applications or evidence of information discussed. We will start with a look at the Pastoral Care system and its current state in education, to set the scene for the rest of the book. Each chapter after has a specific focus to guide you on your pastoral care journey beginning with finding your vision and values before looking at how to develop yourself and secure a pastoral role. Once you are in post, however, is when the real fun begins, and each chapter thereafter aims to instill some advice and guidance on the myriad of responsibilities you will have including leading staff; behaviour management; attendance and punctuality and safeguarding. It wouldn't be a useful book if it didn't also touch on the phenomenally important role partnerships with parents and carers play in the professional life of a member of the pastoral team, or the work you will do with the wider curriculum.

In Pastoral Care the motto of "if you don't laugh, you'll cry" is very often apt and, intermixed with the serious, I have also included some of the many shocking, silly and suspect tales the profession has to offer. It is the work you do, or will do, that will shape the lives of countless young people, and I believe there to be no greater privilege, but gosh do we need to enjoy the journey together!

Pastoral Care was an area of work that I, quite happily, fell into and have loved ever since. I've spent the past fifteen years, after starting as a volunteer, as an ICT Technician, a Teaching Assistant, Head of Careers Education, Assistant Head of Year, Head of Year, Head of Student Support, Boys Champion, Director of Attendance and Punctuality, Head of Key Stage, Assistant Headteacher and now Deputy Headteacher as well as being a Teacher of Business, Computing and Maths. I've also spent the past seven years supporting schools as a primary and secondary school Governor, Member and Chair of Trustees.

This book is written in an unapologetically no-nonsense style – it's my aim for it to be an extension of myself and to be something you could pick up, read for ten minutes and then go and try out whatever you've gleaned. I have found I have gained the most enjoyment, and use, from educational reading which is grounded in the reality of the world we work in and I hope that this book will be a similar proposition, allowing you to take a break from the busy world of pastoral care to reflect on your own practice and journey.

To create environments in which young people flourish and thrive or, in some cases, in which we are the only constant in their difficult lives is a role that should be looked upon with great envy. I am honoured to have worked within this sector for the past 13 years and I hope that whether you are an old-hand, or new to the party, that you do, or will, feel exactly the same.

1 Pastoral Care in Schools (Systems/Roles)

The wonderful thing about Pastoral Care is the diversity found within the system – walk into two schools that are next door to each other and there's every chance you find a pastoral system that is exactly the same or polar opposites. In this chapter, I examine the current position we find ourselves in within the world of pastoral care and the myriad of challenges, roles and opportunities we face.

Changing Definitions of Pastoral Care

I speak very often within this book using the context of England, but this same pattern of differing systems can be observed all over the world. The word 'Pastoral' is one that hasn't quite spread to all reaches of the globe yet in the context of school-based care – originating through religion, the idea of pastoral care is one centred around the development of values often associated with the key principles of religious society.

'Pastoral Care,' as we use the term now, is the safeguarding and development of a child both physically and emotionally. Pastoral Care systems in schools are increasingly all-encompassing with responsibility for driving forward behaviour management, safeguarding, achievement, attendance, mental health and wellbeing and academic attainment. As society finds itself stripped of support through the reduction of public services the onus has very often fallen upon our schools to offer more services to the community.

If you work within a pastoral system, you will likely find yourself swapping between many hats during your working day; social worker; mentor; teacher; police officer; investigator; counsellor; parental advisor and much more. That's not to devalue the professions listed above, all of whom work with us in our roles to ensure that our children are safe and happy, but rather to illustrate the way that pastoral care in schools has changed over time. This is evident in some schools more than others and this begins to explain some of the ways pastoral care has changed over recent years.

The Widening Reach of Pastoral Roles

One area which has seen much change is the roles which fall under the umbrella of Pastoral Care within our schools. We now have a workforce which includes more staff, teaching and non-teaching, in pastoral roles than ever before – schools no longer exist purely as a place of education and the need for these roles is evident. Which of the roles below, or some variation, can be found in your school?

Mentor	Counsellor	Therapist	Head of Year
Assistant Head of Year	Chaplain	Behaviour Manager	Safeguarding Officer
Pastoral Manager	Wellbeing Lead	Careers Advisor	Forest School Leader
Outreach Officer	Matron	Inclusion Manager	EAL Teacher
Houseparent	Academic Mentor	SEMH/EBD Teacher	Art/Music Therapist
Pastoral Administrator	Attendance Leader	On-Call/Duty Manager	Assistant/Deputy Head
Head of House	1-1 support	PP/Disadvantaged Leader/Support/Mentors	

If you are looking for a pastoral role you can begin to decide on a route which suits you and capitalises on your own personal drive and experience – the above is a small sample of the most common roles. I will say however, that every school also has different names for their roles – I've already mentioned in the Introduction that one of my previous roles was as 'Boys Champion' and boy (no pun intended) is that one that gets strange looks when you mention it. For the purposes of this book, I'll let you imagine it was a gladiatorial role in which I was selected to fight off unruly opponents, Gladiator/Game of Thrones style – the reality is only *slightly* tamer.

Evolving Pastoral Roles and Systems

There is a constant developmental churn within pastoral care that necessitates reviewing the systems and roles we have in place in our schools. Much of this should be driven by your context and an analysis of the needs/priorities for pastoral care in your school community. As much as we would love to be able to solve all of society's problems, we simply don't have the capacity, funding or experience to do so.

Increasingly I find myself stretched thinly – covering areas that would never have been dreamed of being a facet of an education provision – within the last four weeks, for example, I've been asked to speak to a housing officer; get in touch with substance abuse professionals and support with investigations being conducted by the police into serious crime. I don't begrudge this – it's what our community needs and the support of trusted professionals in the form of school staff is invaluable for our staff, students and parents. The issue is when we expect our pastoral staff to be all things to everyone.

We must constantly reflect as pastoral staff, leaders and school staff on what are the biggest issues affecting us and how we can work to ensure that our individual systems can cope with these demands. If we know as a school that our pastoral staff are disproportionately dealing with safeguarding issues – what are we doing about it? Does it need a short-term solution of training for staff, talks to students, etc. or is this an ingrained issue that we need to invest time and money into? Do we need to bring in a new role to the school – a support staff Safeguarding Officer to support with the issues we are facing? Are we a part of a trust where central staff could adapt their roles to support in the short term?

These are the kinds of questions you should be asking regularly, drawing information from the contextual data you harvest every day within your pastoral work. I worked in a school in which Heads of Year were members of teaching staff – after a cycle of two rounds of recruitment for the role it was decided that it would be wise to offer a temporary role to non-teaching staff under an honorarium to fill the gap. The role was a great success but when it came time to review it the leadership team felt that, despite this success, they did not want to remove a teaching middle leadership role from the school's TLR structure and so moved again to advertise for a teaching Head of Year. Why? Because it was easier. Was it the right thing for the school community? Probably not.

The Role of Pastoral Care in the Curriculum

It would also be unwise not to focus on where Pastoral Care fits within the curriculum – the current drive for our curriculum and teaching to match our communities' contextual needs should extend to our pastoral care systems – just because the same systems have been in place in a school for an extended period of time doesn't mean that we shouldn't reflect on whether they still meet the needs of the community. The best schools are those who manage to expertly interweave outstanding pastoral care with outstanding teaching and learning – recognising that they are two sides of the same coin. There can sometimes be a conversation around which is needed more to ensure the best possible education for our children but to have that conversation is reductive and doesn't recognise the contribution each has to the other.

Without exceptional standards for behaviour even the best planned, researched and enacted lessons will fall down. Equally, a completely compliant class is no guarantee that learning is taking place – we must develop a balance that gives the best of both worlds. This interweaving of responsibilities extends into much of school life – pastoral care should influence your school's curriculum; it will impact your SEND offer and it will shape your CEIAG provision, to name but a few areas. This is why it's so important that we acknowledge the deeply important role pastoral care plays within our schools beyond just the day-to-day responsive nature of the role.

There are many who would counsel against moving into pastoral care if you hold ambitions of leadership at the highest level – that taking an academic route, curriculum or data would better serve those purposes. This demonstrates the level of feeling towards pastoral care sometimes found and often shows a lack of understanding of the nuance and multi-faceted nature of the field – alongside the development of a skillset which allows you to respond to even the most extreme scenarios with poise and consideration.

Increasing Importance and Influence of Pastoral Care

If we are to reflect on where pastoral care might move in the future we are unlikely to see a world where the demands of the sector decrease – it's more likely that the issues we regularly see coming into school will continue to increase in prevalence. Budgets and finances are like to remain stretched, public services will continue to feel the same pressure and the rise in the influence of social media/the internet/artificial intelligence on the issues we deal with will no doubt continue to cause problems. As pastoral staff we will need to work smarter, not harder, to ensure that the entire system stands the test of time in these scenarios and that we can cope with the ever-evolving needs of the children in our care whilst mitigating for all of the factors working against us – and gosh does that sound difficult.

We need to come together as a sector to demand more for our students and ensure that we can meet their needs – there are so many issues currently at the forefront of education (wellbeing/mental health, behaviour, attendance, etc.), many of which have plenty of government advisors, policies, crackdowns and more attached to them. I'd encourage you to reflect on how you ensure that the voice of your students is heard beyond the walls of your school because there is going to come a time when our pastoral teams can no longer do the vital work done every single day. For some schools, this will already be their reality and for some they won't even know it's coming.

Case Study 1.1 Reviewing Roles – Thoughts on the Most Appropriate Pastoral Roles at Passmores Academy

by Vic Goddard
Co-Principal, Passmores Academy

There is no doubt that our personal experience has an impact on how we view life, and this is not limited to outside the workplace. When I became a dad, it made me look at the big moments in a child's life in a whole different way. You may have seen 1000s of young people transition from primary to secondary school but until you've done it with your first child you really don't know how it feels!

At Passmores we looked at the genuine worries of our youngest students and our desire to create a school that truly feels like a community and moved to a vertical tutoring system. As we already had a house system it made sense to use that to go vertical and move away from Heads of Year to Heads of House. The early teething problems of having to move some of our students to different houses to create the balanced tutor group we needed were soon overcome as the opportunities to develop a sense of belonging and pride in their house took over.

There are many benefits of the change; now 10 years on:

- Breaking down the artificial barriers between year groups especially to parents concerned at transition.
- Enabling each young person to have an older 'learning partner' to support them with day-to-day organisation as well as being able to offer their 'experience' of key school moments, etc.

- A form tutor only ever has to complete five of the more time-consuming tutor reports at any one time.
- House competitions have never been stronger or involved more students.
- Staff know their tutees better than they ever did.
- At key times in the student journey through school such as making option choices we have a programme of assemblies, etc. that leaves only that year group with their tutor to give them as much chance to talk things through as they need.

There are small tweaks that have occurred over the years such as making the school crest on their ties the same colour as their house so we can tell instantly, and to make sure their ties are the right length of course. There have been some changes of late as we recently removed year 11 from the vertical system as the unique challenges they have faced over the last couple of years has meant we wanted to give them a more bespoke pastoral experience.

Overall, the impact of any organisational changes when it comes to pastoral care is wide ranging and can support/alter the ethos in a very distinct way. The house system permeates every aspect of school life and gives each young person the sense of belonging they crave.

Questions about Systems and Roles in Pastoral Care to Ask of Yourself, Your Team, Your Staff, Your Students or Your Wider Community

Are our pastoral systems appropriate for the contextual needs of our school/trust – do we regularly review these needs considering data and the opinion of our stakeholders?

What are the biggest issues facing our pastoral staff, or staff responding to pastoral concerns, and how can we mitigate against these?

Do we regularly make use of student, staff and parent voice to evaluate the success of our pastoral systems?

Are we clear with stakeholders on the purpose of our pastoral systems – do we articulate how pastoral staff operate and the systems within which they are bound?

Do teaching/support staff who aren't part of the pastoral team understand the mechanisms which underpin pastoral care and how they fit into the larger picture?

- How often do we look outward and visit other schools/provisions when we review our pastoral care systems – do we make use of best practise and research or is our response to pastoral care grounded in feeling/sentiment?
- How often do we collaborate with other schools, both similar and different, to build networks and share resources related to pastoral care? Is our collaboration focused only on behaviour or the entirety of the pastoral landscape?
- Are governors/trustees aware of our pastoral care systems and able to articulate how they operate and the challenges they face?
- Do we regularly share successes within our pastoral systems or do we only share negatives?
- Is pastoral care a feature of discussion around curriculum – is the SLT link responsible for curriculum aware of where pastoral care fits into the picture?
- Do our SEND/EAL/LAC etc. provisions link closely and collaborate with our pastoral staff – are there missed opportunities to reduce workload or share expertise?

2 Vision and Values in Pastoral Care

Your school will have a vision; an ethos, a culture and if you are working in the right school for you then your own vision and values will align with these. I can't overstate the importance of understanding these key facets of a school before deciding to join them and also of keeping yourself aware of any changes to them in your current school.

This chapter aims to demystify the corporate jargon and mission statement, with the aid of real-life case studies and contributions, to make clear the need for cultural alignment with your organisation, as well as reflecting on how to understand the needs of your community in setting these key strategic elements.

The Importance of 'Matching' with Your School

If you find yourself in a situation where you don't match with the culture of the school it can often compound the small issues into larger issues – being asked to complete some extra marking as a teaching Head of Year, when you find the marking and assessment policy to be over-complicated and time consuming will only serve to frustrate you – so try and avoid this issue in the first place.

There are always compromises to be made – you are unlikely to find the perfect school where every policy and practise is one that you agree with. I doubt you could even find a Headteacher of a school who feels this way about their own school and at every level there are things that we will find frustrating or disagreeable. You need to decide on the things that you believe to be non-negotiable and ensure that when doing your due diligence on a school these are the areas you pay particular attention to. *The following case study is my own personal reflection of a difficult time in which a school that I had moved to changed, almost overnight, through new leadership and the reflection I had to undertake in deciding whether it still reflected the same vision and values that drew me to it.*

> **Case Study 2.1 Mismatched Cultures and Goals: A Prime Example**
>
> As Senior Student Support Officer my role was to support the pastoral care needs of the school and be the 'front-line' for pastoral care needs within Key Stage Four. I'd joined this school around 2.5 years earlier as an Assistant Head of Year and worked my way through Head of Year and into the role I now found myself in. During this time the Headteacher left, and the school was brokered into a trust after an Inadequate Ofsted judgement. I had moved to the school to get experience in pastoral care and boy did it deliver – I don't think I've ever worked in such a fast-moving, difficult pastoral environment due to the context of the school at the time.
>
> The benefit of this was that I was exposed to a great deal of incidents, issues and opportunities that never would have fallen at my feet elsewhere. I had developed an affinity for the school and the students within it and felt a deep desire to be a part of the journey to wrench the school out of the mire and back to a position where it's rating matched the work put in by staff. The brokering into a trust brought with it a new Headteacher who immediately sought to crackdown on behaviour – the right move for the school and something that was much needed.
>
> Unfortunately, in doing this the Headteacher changed my role from one which was previously focused on a wide variety of pastoral areas into a purely firefighting behaviour role – the student support team were timetabled to be on given corridors/floors for much of the day and the role became one where every interaction, with every student was a negative one. Picking up the pieces of an issue in a lesson, escorting them to the removal room, collecting detentions, responding to issues at break/lunch etc.
>
> The role changed so significantly that this school, in which I felt only a few months earlier that I would be in it for the long-haul and a part of the drive forward, became somewhere I dreaded coming to. I'll make the point again that this was needed, it was a direction that I agreed with, but I didn't want my every interaction with students to be negative, particularly in what I felt was such a formative point in my own career, and I made the decision to resign a couple of months later. I make this point because it illustrates just how quickly a situation can change around you and how aware you have to be of the shifting sands beneath your feet.

The Importance of Clear Vision and Values

Every school has a catchy slogan in today's modern world of education whether it's 'Building Brighter Futures' or 'Achieving Aspiration for All'– most schools also have a set of values now that are vaunted, 'Respectful, Committed, Confident', and are usually stuck up in vinyl on some corridors. That sounds like I'm being critical – on the contrary – schools with a clear vision/values that are lived by the community and relentlessly pushed by staff tend to do very well. Where they hold meaning and link directly to the aims of the school/trust they offer an exceptional opportunity to encapsulate the drive and mission of the school and offer clear guidelines for students to follow.

'Work Hard, Be Kind' is a popular value statement seen in a wide variety of schools – I use this example because it's easy to communicate with students and they understand it's meaning. It can equally be weaved into the conversation in all facets of school life. I clearly remember the values of my own secondary school education as they were drilled into us at every opportunity – the focus of the assembly calendar, referenced in newsletters, part of conversations around behaviour/aspiration and more. There are schools I have worked in, where it was my job to reflect the values of the organisation, which I remember less clearly!

Marketing Ploy or Genuine Aspiration

The issue I take is when these values statements are purely for marketing purposes – if your students don't know what your values statements are or can't articulate them clearly or how they apply to the school, then they are nothing more than a marketing ploy. Your job when looking at potential schools, or if you are in a position looking at your own schools' vision/values, is to try and determine which category they fall into. One clear example that stands out in my head is that I love the idea of outreach, charity work, extra-curricular activity and fundraising within schools – it's important to me that the school I work in feels the same. I believe it's a huge benefit for students and helps to develop them into the rounded individuals I spoke about earlier. If I see that a school I am interested in applying to pushes itself as having similar values, then they immediately interest me more.

It took me a few years to realise how important it was to 'match' with your school. You can describe it as 'being on the bus' – are you heading in the same direction and is everybody aware of where they are going? Make sure that you are also aware if the bus takes a sharp left or heads in a different direction – this might be time to get off!

The Value of Constant Reiteration to Staff, Students and the wider community

It's the role of the school then to ensure that staff/students can talk the talk - as an outsider to a school if you tell me that all of your student's are 'Community Champions' then I'd expect you, and them, to be able to tell me what that means and how that translates into the lived experience of students in the school. On an interview day I had just that opportunity – a school which stated that charity was at its heart but when I took the opportunity to speak to students about it they were none the wiser. That doesn't mean the school isn't, perhaps, doing a great job of achieving their charitable/community aims but it does mean that they likely aren't articulating this clearly enough to students and guiding them in why it's so important. Overcommunicate your values, vision and expectations – there is no downside to this. We want our students and staff to be able to articulate the 'why' of working at/learning at our school and the only way you can get everybody on the same page is by constantly re-iterating why we do what we do.

The Possibility and Practise of Influencing or Changing Values

There is always the opportunity to influence the values of the school you work in and change culture from within, also. This will differ depending on your role and the remit you have to enact change, but we can all play our part. Ultimately, it is the decision of the schools governing body/board of trustees to decide on the vision of the school, and its associated values, and this will usually be driven by the Headteacher and leadership team. If that's you then I'd encourage you to look at the values you purport to be present/ visible within your school and make a judgement about whether they are simply a nice thing to put onto your headed paper or whether they are truly embedded into the culture of the school. Student voice should allow you to interrogate whether this is the case.

It may be that you have too many values or statements and they all blur into one; it may be that the values you have chosen don't match the drives/ needs of the community/local context or even that you simple haven't put in enough opportunities for them to be explicitly communicated. Does every member of staff understand the school's values? How do they, in turn, communicate these with student and parents?

Considering the Needs of Your School Community

Think about your local context – if one of your values is Ambition and you work in a disadvantaged environment in which 'Ambition' is a buzzword for going to university is there a better word to encapsulate this mission? At a previous school parents believed 'Ambition' was something reserved for the upper class and that their children just needed to work hard – something they themselves did. Working hard obviously is a means to achieving your ambitions but this message resonated much more. Flip the context to one without disadvantage where 'working hard' means working yourself to the bone – we've all worked with students whose parents insist they come home from school and work all evening. Is 'Work Hard' the right message to send here? As with everything – look to the needs of your community and reflect upon which message will resonate.

The remainder of this chapter features contributions from four Headteachers/ex-headteachers reflecting on the importance of vision and values within their own schools and the work that they have done to achieve this. In reading them you will see that, very often, the only link between their very successful school cultures is a focus on achieving the best for their own communities via delving into the heart of what they need, and understanding the key elements necessary for success within each. They decide what is important to them (often shaped by their experiences), link it to what is important within their school communities or context, and then live these values every day of their working lives through every interaction with every stakeholder in their communities.

Thank you to Halil, Phil, Ges and Mark – all of whom have transformed the culture of their schools through this forensic focus on finding out *exactly* what their community needed, from individual interactions to whole-school developments.

Case Study 2.2 Building Belonging

by Halil Tamgumus
Headteacher, Braunstone Community Primary School

I walked into the school halfway through the academic year. I walked in as a new headteacher (my first headship post), into a school where the staff did not know me and where the children did not care to know me. I was fine with this - I had not earnt their trust or respect yet.

I was not worried walking into the school – the school had a bad reputation mainly because of where it is. If the rumours about the area were to be believed most people would have hesitated walking into the building – but not me.

I grew up on the estate. It was like coming home.

I walked down one of the corridors and saw a group of year 6 boys milling around – there were 5 of them. It was lunchtime and the sun was out, but they were not. By the time I got to about 5 meters from them a member of staff had already spotted them and began yelling at them for not following the school rules.

"Why are you not outside? Why are you in here? You shouldn't be in here! OUT!"

Not once did the staff member pause between the questions to get an understanding of why they were inside. Not once did I hear the boys talk. They shuffled closer together and walked down the corridor in unison, heads down.

I caught up with them outside.

ME:	"Boys. You alright?"
	Nods all round but when I looked into their eyes all I could see was sadness. The weight of the world on their shoulders.
ME:	"Why were you inside?"
ONE OF THE BOYS:	"We were bored sir. We don't feel like playing outside"
	It is important to mention that the boys were all non-white. This matters.
ME:	"Boys, it's clear that you shouldn't be in. Why is today different? Why are you bored today?"
BOYS:	(Shrugs)
ME:	"Look, come and sit down with me and we'll chat about it. Maybe we can change things, so you are not so bored. (whispering) Also the real reason I want to sit down is because I am getting old"
	The boys laughed at this.
ME:	"and because it's the first day of Ramadan and I am tired already!"
	All off a sudden, the boys backs straightened, and they were looking at each other with wide eyes and open mouths – shocked. Internally I started to panic – what have I said? Did I accidently swear without knowing? Was there something hanging out of my nose?
	One of the boys stepped forward "Sir, are you Muslim?"

ME: "Yes – I am Turkish Cypriot – why?"
THE BOY: "We're Muslim too sir, we are fasting too"

I soon discovered the children had not told anyone (staff or children) that they were fasting – they never shared the fact that they were Muslim. When I asked them why this was they told me it was because they were worried about being bullied – "It's hard enough being black sir, if they knew we were Muslim too – phew!"

Needless to say, my first assembly started with – "Good morning everyone, my name is Mr Tamgumus and some of you may already know that I am a Muslim…"

During that Ramadan, I got to know the boys well, they would come into my office, and we would chat about anything and everything. Football, the kind of foods they like to eat, the languages they spoke at home. They needed to feel they were part of something, accepted, seen as different but respected for it at the same time. I know what this feels like. I grew up with the same wants and desires from education too.

To belong. It is one of our 4 key words. Our Ethos and Values which we live every day.

Belong, Care, Persevere, Succeed

Case Study 2.3 Values Driven Education

by Phil Jones
National Chair for The National Association for Pastoral Care in Education
Educational Consultant and Former Headteacher

As a Headteacher and consultant I have been privileged to work with many schools and communities – an incredibly proud moment was in developing a Learning Centre to provide additional capacity for the pastoral care and support for young people in schools across a local community. The vision was that young people could be supported in their education and personal development, by establishing a centre that could use available resources, to target support and interventions, to respond to different needs. This was based on a set of values; that young people should always be treated with respect, that they learn from adults being positive role models, and that they should be responsible for their behaviour and attitudes and have opportunities to reflect and learn from their actions.

The plan was that a school that was closing, because of a temporary reduction in school numbers in an area, could be used to provide additional capacity for schools to reduce exclusions and provide targeted support and interventions for learners. The vision was based on the belief that The Learning Centre would make a real difference in the educational experience and future life chances of the young people enrolled there. This was important because it was challenging to persuade the local authority that it was a cost-effective use of the buildings. It appeared nobody had ever suggested not boarding a school building up while it was not needed, even though the site would be required as a school in the future. It was also important to have a clear vision to persuade the schools that it could be a cost-effective way of increasing the capacity to support learners.

The Learning Centre was established with a small staff, who because of the clear vision and values about its purpose were fully committed to making it successful. There were no resources available, so we used donated paint to paint the rooms ourselves and this gave us a shared sense of purpose and a belief in the values. One day another Headteacher came in to see me as Head of the Learning Centre and did not recognise me in my overalls doing the painting. This was an important part of the values that the team shared, that nobody was more important to the team than anybody else. This had an important impact on the culture and ethos that was created for the young people who came to the centre. I told the staff that when it went well, they could be proud of their achievements and when it went wrong it was my fault as the leader.

A part of the work of the Learning Centre was the 'Independent Learning Zone' which took learners at risk of exclusion for short-term placements to find ways to engage them in learning again. The name was important because its purpose was to support individuals to cope with their difficulties, that were preventing them from learning and not to simply punish them, which in truth was what the schools expected and wanted when we first opened. The staff were committed to the vision, and it became clear that we were all trying too hard because we wanted it to be a success. We were spending too much time checking that the individual learners were on task, and this was not going to be the reality when they returned to their classrooms and was not helping them to be independent learners. The staff commitment to the vision, meant that we spent time at the end of the day reflecting on our experience, so we could improve the support we were providing for learners. There was a clear understanding that staff had to be positive role models and that if young people did not meet expectations, there would be a consequence, but they would always be welcome back to a fresh start the next day. Young people were always treated with respect, and it was made clear that the staff's motivation, was to help them become more successful learners.

There were many challenging days, but the staff were encouraged by positive feedback from schools and parents, that time spent in the Independent Learning

Centre had been a positive experience, that had focused the young people, on what they needed to do to achieve more success from their education. Many of the young people did not want to leave the Learning Centre, to return to their schools, at the end of their placement, as they had felt valued and that they had made progress. They often came back to visit to see the staff and share their growing confidence in their ability to be successful. The Learning Centre was open for nearly three years, until the site was needed again for a school. Hundreds of young people benefited from the support that was provided and it is probably true that the impact the Learning Centre made was only fully appreciated after it closed.

Case Study 2.4 Community Ownership

by Ges Smith
Headteacher, London Secondary School

In 2011 I was lucky enough to go to New York as part of the Future Leaders Programme. I was a Pastoral Deputy at my school and embraced the opportunity to experience first-hand the work and ethos of the charter schools we visited. New York was obviously amazing and the work these schools did was also hugely impressive. But what struck me and many of the other school leaders on the trip was how explicit the vision and values message was within the schools themselves. It was "in your face" branding which you could not avoid experiencing in every part of the school environment. If I saw "Reach for the Stars" once, I saw it a dozen times.

On my return, I knew that my school needed to consider its vision and values message and how it underpinned our work in a challenging urban environment. I also knew what I did not want from the American model which sometimes left me feeling like I had just entered a cult. My aim was an explicit message about our ethos, values and aspiration for the students. It needed to be embedded in all aspects of school life and be relevant and accessible to all members of our school community. To cut a very long story short, many months of consultation and collaboration resulted in the birth of the ACHIEVE agenda which to this day underpins the amazing work the school does. The agenda is now a fundamental part of our reward system, assembly and tutor time programme, branding, social media profile, uniform and values system.

In February 2018, I took up an Executive Headship with another local school which was experiencing significant change and challenge at senior leadership level. I have to be honest; I took a great deal of pride in establishing ACHIEVE at my own school, but knew there was a real challenge in establishing a similar vision and values identity in a church school that I had not been part of establishing and which had not previously embraced the need to celebrate and share its unique identity and value set. I knew the task would stretch my leadership skills to ensure the whole school community had a sense of ownership and it was not just me driving my agenda and my ideas.

One of the most challenging parts was tying in the Christian ethos into the work we were doing and keeping all stakeholders on board with the messages we wanted to deliver. The answer lay in the structure and input from the working group who drove the project. It soon became obvious that my group had to be made up from representatives of the whole school community and had to give each of those people a real voice. The real eye-opener for me was how we were able to find a common ground to work the Christian ethos into our message and still retain the strength of clear principles that were relevant to an urban school in challenging circumstances. The majority of our students and staff did not follow the Christian faith yet the resultant "Believe, Grow, Succeed" resonated with everyone and did not prompt a single complaint or concern.

It is now firmly embedded in the school's culture and one of my proudest moments was to have it directly referenced in the first paragraph of the school's OFSTED report as an indication of the positive direction the school was now taking following a challenging few years. It reinforced my belief, albeit a slightly cliched one, that as we lead we learn to adapt and develop our approaches to achieve the best outcomes.

Case Study 2.5 Changing Lives

by Mark Oldman
Executive Principal

The academic year of 2016/17 will go down as the hardest of my career so far, performing the role of Executive Head over two schools brings about a funny mix of guilt, excitement, frustration, pride and loneliness. That being said, it also turned out to be the most successful; outstanding Ofsted inspections in both schools; numbers on roll at a record high, giving us the chance to reach more families and all of that alongside the best set of exam results the school have ever seen.

Why then was I left with the same question remaining as usual – how do we change a life?

Let me tell you about one of our year 11 leavers from that year, he came to us as a Year 7 on an emergency assessment place and as a child in crisis. When I went to visit him at the city PRU, he was wild, like the Tasmanian devil, scared, vulnerable and determined to run. As far as I saw it taking him onto our roll was an absolute must, even without a formally structured plan, he started the following day.

Day 1 he was living with his Dad and, within 15 minutes of arriving, had punched the ICT teacher and sat on top of the roof, these types of behaviour went on for his first four weeks and sporadically for the next three years. Parent interaction was minimal, we had no back up on detentions and no attendance at arranged meetings to discuss his behaviour and a joint plan for change. Left in the hands of the school and our family support team we started to get to know the child, he needed love and care and self-belief, his confidence had been quashed, or had never truly been there, and he was living a life with no barriers but was absolutely desperate for warmth and guidance. We went for a multi-faceted approach, rapid and regular literacy intervention would kickstart his ability to access the curriculum and hopefully add to his confidence; daily swimming trips based on good behaviour let him know that we meant what we said and that we enjoyed his company and an unlikely friend arrived in his year group and the continued improvement of the school meant better and better staff flooded in to offer support.

On an almost three-monthly cycle he faltered, his actions and attitude asked questions of our behaviour policy and questioned my own commitment to believing that relationships were everything. Sometimes he infuriated me, sometimes I wanted to laugh, but mostly I couldn't shake the opportunity that presented itself when we first met, here was a life that needed a platform for change and that needed our school.

If he struggled in lessons we put in more support – less contact from home meant more visits to home and we did everything we could to provide wrap-around opportunities – trips out at the weekends and holidays and more nights in residence with people who believed in him. By this time, he was living with his mum, his appearance had become unkempt and he was acting as a carer for his niece, we knew all of this because he had finally started to open up and he knew we believed in him.

As we approached the end of year 11, he began to see what a talented and intelligent young man he was, some confidence was restored and some belief in people had started to be cultivated, he had established meaningful enduring relationships with key people around the school, the English and Arts teachers had unlocked something very special, and we could tell he might have established some self-worth and drive. He excelled during the exam period and had started to commit to further study, he had let us know that home was hard, and that social care were back involved, he was vulnerable and scared again so we made sure we saw him every week during the holidays and tried to offer a path through.

With a sneaky peak at results the day before he got them, both me and my Deputy Heads knew, he was our most successful pupil ever! His results transcended anything we had seen before and the look on his face was priceless, we all spent the day fighting back the tears, he opened the results without family but with every member of staff present and on tenterhooks. The frustration and the beauty in schools like ours is that you have the privilege to know the whole child, their journeys, their battles and hopefully their dreams, one of the hardest factors is that you know the process will start again with a younger pupil the next year, it's already happened this week.

We know we have some key ingredients now that we cannot negotiate on, structure, consistency, engaging and creative people, love, care and personal investment, the ability to digest the journey of a child, no matter how fractured and project them into a future that they will be proud of. My closing speech at inset this year concentrated on what I believe to be the moral obligation that comes with a school like ours and the opportunities it offers. We spoke about the resources that we have and the privilege we have to be able to reach the lives that need it most. I made it clear that we must offer the opposite to the lack of boundaries, consistency, and love, that some of the most vulnerable children in our school are exposed to.

There is nothing quite like experiencing, through the eyes of a child, the most momentous, fantastic memories, or moments after years of struggle. Working in pastoral care gives you the ability to create that one moment, one memory that a young person can always go back to and say, 'that school believed in me, that person cared, that experience helped me to change my life'.

If you are not a leader with direct involvement in deciding vision/values then think carefully about your own school's values – do you understand them? Do you see them lived within the school? Are they built into the narrative of conversations with stakeholders? How can you contribute to building their profile? Sometimes it is as simple as being a teacher, in a lesson, and referring to one of the school's values in a link to the work/topic you are covering.

As a pastoral member of staff, it can be about building those values into the language you use with students. If 'Work Hard, Be Kind' is the overarching value set of the school then it's really easy if you are called to deal with an incident to use this specific language and adapt it to the situation – "Mr Jones has asked me to come and speak to you because you haven't completed any work today" becomes "Mr Jones has asked me to come and speak to you because you haven't been working hard today – that's one of the things we ask of you at this school". Starting an assembly about anti-bullying can easily be adapted to include a reference to the fact that "at our school we are kind... and I know that each of you is a kind and caring member of our community". Just by adapting our language we re-enforce the values of the school and we start to drip-feed our expectations into the minds of our students, and often staff at the same time.

To leave anyone in doubt about what you value is opening the door for speculation – as schools we must be clear, beyond any doubt, what it is we stand for. Don't let anyone else fill in the gaps – make it so abundantly obvious what your values are and live them every day.

Questions (about Vision and Values in Pastoral Care?) to Ask of Yourself, Your Team, Your Staff, Your Students or Your Wider Community

What is my own vision for pastoral care?

What are the values I hold closest to me and how do these impact me in my role?

What do I believe is the purpose of pastoral care?

Can I clearly identify the vision/values of the school I work in? Do they match with my own vision/values?

As a school, are our vision and values clearly communicated to all members of the community?

Are the community consulted on changes to our vision and values – do they understand why we have made changes if we have to?

How do we communicate this and how do we know that the message is heard?

How often do we communicate our vision/values and the reasoning behind this?

What do we do to ensure that those students/staff/parents who are new to our community understand our vision/values?

How do we measure whether our vision/values are the lived experience of those in the school? Does student and staff voice take place with this as a focus?

What do we want our students to remember about our school?

3 Developing Pastoral Care Experience

When it comes to any role it's usually a good idea to try and develop some experience in that area before you dive into the water, or, in the case of pastoral care, headfirst into the shark-infested waters below. That isn't to make pastoral care sound scary or more difficult to work within than it is but merely an acknowledgement that jumping straight in with no experience of pastoral care whatsoever is likely to cause you more problems than doing so with even the smallest amount of gathered experience.

Fortunately for most of us already working in schools the opportunities to develop experience are often freely available and, even if they aren't, every member of staff in a school has some form of pastoral care responsibility whether that it is a duty to follow safeguarding practise, operating as a form tutor, talking to parents on the phone etc. When seeking out extra opportunities to gather this experience, there are a multitude of options that are available to us.

In this chapter I explore some time-tested strategies to develop your pastoral care experience, some that I undertook myself when breaking into pastoral care and others that I have overseen as the 'mentor' rather than 'mentored'.

The Power of Shadowing Colleagues

Shadowing your colleagues can be an excellent introduction to pastoral care roles – and frankly when you see the work that these staff put in behind the scenes it will give you a new understanding of the world you are hoping to enter. Think carefully about what kind of role you are looking for and who the best person to approach may be – if you enjoy solving problems with children and being a confidante, then shadowing a no-nonsense sergeant-major type may not be the best person for you. If you know you wish to progress into a leadership role then finding someone with similar ambitions who could guide you on a similar path would be a good start. Broadly speaking, find the person you feel is most aligned with your own direction.

The first option available to you for gaining experience is to use the primary pastoral care resource available to you – the people already doing the job. There's a lot to learn as a member of pastoral staff in any role and unless you have a completely new team around you there will be a wealth of experience on offer. Pastoral staff use a range of tools from a toolkit developed over time and through well-honed practice to navigate even the most unpredictable days. Spend some time observing and watching, whether that's from afar or up close, and decide where you need to develop your experience or understanding.

That isn't to say you can't also develop pastoral experience from members of staff who aren't in pastoral roles either. If you are a teacher struggling with keeping students calm in detentions, something you will almost certainly need to be able to do if taking up a pastoral role, ask for strategies from others in your faculty team who you've seen do this well – pastoral care crosses the boundaries of all school roles and there is knowledge to be gained from them all. The crucial thing here is to make sure you do this with a specific focus as it will make it much easier for you to analyse what makes the member of staff good at what they do. If you don't have a specific focus before you beginning shadowing/observing the likelihood is you will walk away from it no clearer about the skills/strategies they use.

I was fortunate to spend time as an Assistant Head of Year to some excellent and experienced HOYs and so was exposed to best practise when it came to running meetings, speaking to students, resolving issues, talking to parents and more. For example, if observing a meeting it would be easy to get caught up in the content of the meeting rather than the order, flow and control – if you know that you are observing the meeting chair's ability to move the meeting along and keep to time then you can start to formulate questions and you'll start to pick out specifics.

A Formal or Informal Arrangement?

If you have a good relationship with a member of staff you wish to shadow then asking to informally shadow them, or offer them some support if you have the time, is a nice way to dip your toe into the water without making anything formal. The downside of any informal arrangement is that your ambition to move into a pastoral role may go unnoticed by staff responsible for internal appointments.

If you want to go through a more formal route, and make your intentions known, then book a meeting with whoever leads the pastoral team, cleared through your own line manager first, and ask if there is any opportunity to shadow or support the pastoral team. The worst they can say is no. Very often in schools we don't know other people's ambitions unless they tell us first – when I applied for my first Head of Year position the Headteacher said that she hadn't even considered me as an option and didn't think it would be something I'd be interested in.

Shadowing may also bring more concrete opportunities – lots of schools have voluntary roles that relate to pastoral care – assistant heads of year, house champions, mentors, etc. If your school doesn't have one of these perhaps you could suggest it as a means to develop your experience and benefit the school at the same time. Even just making your desire to get into pastoral care known may open up some opportunities for development that previously weren't there – bear in mind that any formal approach may make it harder to drop whatever you have started if you decide it isn't for you.

Tapping Into The Wider School Community

Another vital step to securing/developing your pastoral care experience is to see the work undertaken by other schools/professionals. One of the experiences which shaped one of my core beliefs, that extracurricular/co-curricular activity is fundamental to the success of a school and the inculcation of an excellent culture, was a visit to an outstanding school early on in my career. They had a reputation for success with boys from a similar context to ours and it became clear immediately that they used their extracurricular success, and wide offering, to instill a sense of pride and teamwork within their school community, who all beamed about the provision when it was discussed. These kinds of experiences can provide you with lifelong learning – I'm pleased to say that this visit, so early on in my career, then became a cornerstone of my practice as an Assistant Headteacher, when I was gifted the opportunity to transform Co-curricular provision as part of a team improving an Inadequate school to help give students a sense of belonging and care for their culture and community. Opportunities like this are plentiful and, with the rise of leaders on social media offering their school's time and resources to interested parties, easier than ever to arrange.

You just need to think about how any visit could provide a positive impact on your school and take the suggestion to your line manager/Head.

Fundamentally, Pastoral leadership (I use the phrase leadership here as I believe that anybody working in pastoral care is thrust so often into the unexpected that leadership is a trait often utilised) often depends upon your ability to 'hold the line' and insist upon the highest standards. Anybody looking to develop pastoral care experience in the pursuit of a pastoral role must ensure that any areas you are already responsible for are led with the highest standards possible.

> **Case Study 3.1 Pastoral care in the classroom**
>
> by Laura Acton
> Senior Leader, Parliament Hill Girl's School, Camden, London
>
> Perhaps like most secondary teachers I wanted to teach because of a love of my subject (Drama). I hadn't foreseen the amount of an impact pastoral care would have on my teaching and classroom practice. I also hadn't considered how much time outside of the classroom I would spend thinking about my students, their well-being, their work, their performances and how to get the best out of them. Performing and participating in Drama can feel exposing and I soon realised that unless students feel safe, they will never be able to fully partake and engage to reach their potential. At the core of my practice has been aiming to create an inclusive space to ensure that students feel like they belong in the room so that they feel confident enough to make contributions. I am lucky that there are excellent pastoral systems in place in my school which means that as a teacher I can concentrate on encouraging students to collaborate, feel invested in their work, and have genuine agency in the creation of theatre and performance.
>
> I have often been left bemused at reactions when I tell new people I meet that I am a teacher, they then ask if it's primary or secondary school and when I respond with secondary it can be met with anything from a compassionate head-tilt to an outright piteous disgusted scrunch of the face. I wonder if it's because most people recall, (perhaps with a certain amount of horror) the often-embarrassing changes that come with becoming a teenager. Secondary students must negotiate puberty, managing hormones, exam pressures and often difficult changing relationships with family and friends. There are so many 'firsts' that happen in those few years and our roles in school can be crucial in supporting students process all this when their emotional maturity is developing. Understandably students are often not equipped with the emotional

literacy to be able to identify and regulate their own moods and feelings and stress. Some students display overt signals that they need additional pastoral support or intervention, for others it may be subtle changes for us to notice and respond to.

If there is a barrier to students being able to engage in their learning and behaviour is poor one of the most obvious things to say (but definitely worth repeating) is that it's the behaviour that is problematic and never the child. Separating the two and making that distinction is essential. It's rare, in fact I cannot think of a single occasion when a student flare-up, or outburst isn't because of something troubling them that feel they have no control over. On those occasions where the behaviour a student displays is a choice, and there are occasions where this is true, we can often dig deeper and find some resulting cause also. Responding with kindness and compassion and helping students to navigate complex emotions has to be one of the most rewarding elements of the job.

Students that could benefit from intervention may not seek it out and might desperately try and hide that something is amiss, perhaps believing that teachers can't help them, or that their problems are too big or too small. Recently a 6th form student reminded me of a time years ago when she was in Year 8 having a tough time, I only see key stage three students for an hour a week but had noticed a change in her participation in class, she usually relished at leading group work and sharing her ideas and she was instead quiet and withdrawn. As she recalls I mentioned to her that she didn't seem like her usual self, and I attempted a light-hearted cajole to encourage her. All these years later she thanked me and disclosed that at the time she was grieving the loss of her grandfather. Apparently I was the only teacher that had noticed. It made me feel proud that I had demonstrated in a very small way that I knew her well enough to see a change, so she felt like she mattered. It made my heart swell to know that I could have made a difference to how she felt for the better that day. It gave me a real sense of pride and a spring in my step however the self-congratulatory imaginary pat on the back faded when I thought about how many other students I might have missed.

There is no blueprint for pastoral care and one size certainly does not fit all but recognising the essential role that we all play in potentially being able to be that consistent and compassionate adult that can support, and nurture, is something to continue to aspire to. We are a valuable resource that could support a young person to navigate their tempestuous teenage years, that has to be considered an honour worthy of a smile rather than a piteous grimace.

Pastoral Care roles can capture the attention of anyone – do any of the questions below resonate with you, if in the given roles, then perhaps Pastoral Care would be for you and you don't even know it. I certainly didn't expect to move into pastoral care when I was working as a Teaching Assistant!

Are you a Teaching Assistant? Do you ensure you support the highest standards in classrooms? Do you deal with negative behaviours in the corridor if you come across them? How do you correct poor behaviour to support/with the support of the class teacher? How do you contribute to whole-school behaviour outside of the classroom?

Are you a class teacher? Are the standards in your classroom high? Do you ensure that the rules of the school are followed? How do you behave on duty? Do you check uniforms as a tutor? Are you confident/comfortable in discussing issues with parents? Are you diligent in your reporting of safeguarding issues? Do you try to support pastoral staff when issues arise?

Are you a mentor working with vulnerable or underachieving students? How do you manage the role of caring/supportive mentor with a need to ensure school rules are followed? How do you support high standards of behaviour in lessons/around school? What strategies have you used to bring about improvements in students' attendance/behaviour/achievement/wellbeing, etc.?

Are you a member of lunchtime support staff? Do you ensure high standards of behaviour at lunchtime? Do you work with other duty staff to ensure consistent responses to behaviour? Do you work to build relationships with students you see regularly?

Are you an IT Technician? Do you understand how IT supports the curriculum? How do you deal with safeguarding issues that arise within the school's IT Network? Do you take opportunities to interact with students/support in lessons? Do you do duties in school – how do you support high standards/expectations around the school?

I have deliberately aimed for a broad field of school roles here because there is potentially a pastoral career ahead of anyone. For me, I have undertaken all of the above roles and could tell you something from each that prepared me for life in pastoral leadership. It's also worth pointing out that some of the best pastoral staff I've worked with have been career changers – from those joining after a career in the army to office staff. We need more and more great *people* working with our children and, whatever your background, there's a world full of opportunity in pastoral care.

Whatever your current role you should be preparing yourself to be a pastoral leader and sweating the small stuff – it doesn't make it any easier, particularly internally, if you have to reset staff and student opinions of you and 'become' a pastoral leader who is reliable and brings assurance. From the moment you step foot into a school have the highest expectations for the children in it, no matter the context, and whatever steps you take on your journey into pastoral roles will be made all the simpler. Remember that as a pastoral leader you are the standard bearer – staff and students will look to you to get things right. They will bring you the things that worry them the most and they need to have confidence that you will address it. If staff lack confidence in your abilities or your response to pastoral issues, they will stop bringing them to you, which brings all manner of issues itself.

Further Ways To Develop Your Experience

Another key strategy to build your pastoral experience is to take up opportunities to be involved in the wider pastoral care of the school. Developing a role in improving and monitoring behaviour, standards, attendance, punctuality etc. for an individual or a group of students is a great thing to be able to discuss when applying for any pastoral role and will build a skillset that ultimately delivers impact. You may do this already if you are a teacher (as a tutor or class teacher perhaps) or mentor but there is a different dynamic to be had when taking a student on report to you that you don't already have an existing relationship with, for example.

A huge part of pastoral care comes down to relationships and building strong, trusting relationships with pupils with a wide variety of needs. Every student needs a different level of support and will require a myriad of strategies, some successful and some not, to address the problems they are having in/out of school. There will also be lots of opportunities within education to develop your pastoral skills through whole school events, running clubs/extra-curricular groups, supporting with duties and much more. I have always enjoyed supporting Duke of Edinburgh events/residentials as it provides an opportunity to see students away from the school environment and any activities of a similar vein help to add experience to your portfolio and increase your chances of securing pastoral care roles – they also provide further opportunity to identify interests, hobbies and motivations for students in your care. The following case study is my own experience and example of how simply taking an interest in a student can bring a wealth of pastoral care experience into your world.

Case Study 3.2 Gaining Confidence in Applying Newly Learnt Pastoral Care Skills

Josh was a Year 9 student with a difficult family life – his parents had gone through a complicated split and him and his two siblings, of which he was the oldest, were finding it difficult to engage with school at a time when their world was collapsing. Josh was one of the first students I worked with as a Boys Mentor – at the time I picked him up his behaviour was the worst in his year group, and he was racking up more behaviour points than any other student. When I first met him, as tends to happen, I couldn't understand how such a pleasant, polite young man could be in such a position.

There is no shortcut when it comes to building trusting relationships and Josh was no exception to this rule, although our relationship did grow faster than many others as he was desperate to offload all of the thoughts circling in his head. After a few meetings with Josh, whose behaviour was poor across the board, we picked out that he hated music with a passion and his behaviour in this lesson was awful. He had music period 1, once a week. He would be removed from his lesson each week and then would go on to have a horrendous day.

Sometimes the best solution is the simplest, Occam's Razor, and I made the decision that we were going to find a way to take Josh out of music rather than try to solve the problem, even though there was resistance to him dropping a subject. I spoke to the Head of DT, who Josh had a good relationship with, and asked if we could get him working in a Year 7 lesson as a technician during this time and both he and Josh loved the idea. We dropped music and he picked up a role supporting younger students in a subject in which he was confident and doing well.

The change in him was almost instant – no behaviour points in any lessons and he was a happy, confident young man whose attitude changed completely. I've never worked with a student since where the solution was so simple and the change so dramatic. It won't always be that simple, or possible, with students you work with but if Josh is any example then if the opportunity presents itself it's worth a try.

Regarding the case study here – don't be afraid to suggest intervention or support ideas you may have whatever your role may be – a member of staff who wants to contribute to pastoral care and believes they have something to offer will often be snapped up! This will further show you are trying to branch out and may make leaders aware of your intentions to move into the sector.

Working Out Your Why

The final piece of advice I would give here whilst developing experience is for you to 'Work Out Your Why'. Pastoral care is very different in different schools, contexts and settings and each role is not created the same. You need to do your research and try and figure out what it is that appeals to you about Pastoral Care. This is about reflecting on your own personal reasons for choosing this path – what are the experiences that have shaped your understanding of Pastoral Care and how do you want to contribute and lead within the sector yourself?

I believe that we owe it to all students to deliver an education system that is predicated upon high standards of both education and pastoral care – I've seen firsthand the impact when this isn't the case and students who have cried out for structure, consistency, and calm. It's no coincidence that when I reflect upon those students who have gone on to find themselves in the most awful situations; prison; murder; assaults and thefts, to name a few, they have come from those educational settings where pastoral care, and the wider culture of the school as a result, failed them. That's not to say that there aren't cases where we fight against a story that feels as if it has already been told and there would have been nothing that could have changed it, but we have a duty, the most important in the world I believe, to ensure that students leave our schools and join the wider world as rounded individuals who have been shaped into kind, morally driven and inquisitive young people.

Case Study 3.3 Progression, Promotion and Prosperity

by Jill Berry
Former Headteacher, Leadership Development Consultant

I had a thirty-year career in schools, during which I held teaching and leadership positions across six different schools: state and independent; all boys', all girls', and co-ed; selective and comprehensive; 4–18, 7–18 and 11–18 schools. I had seven different jobs, as I was internally promoted in my first school. I also taught GCSE and A level to adults at night school, did one-to-one tuition and was an external exam marker and moderator for several years. I feel fortunate and privileged to have had such a range of experiences and opportunities. Teaching is an amazing job – draining and challenging at times, but so worthwhile. And I loved headship most of all.

When I started teaching, people talked about choosing either the pastoral or the academic 'ladder'. I still hear that phrase today and have to say I think it's unhelpful. I held both pastoral and academic leadership roles at different times. I learnt and grew in all of them, and the range of experience definitely made me a better head, in due course. I had credibility, confidence, and a depth of understanding, as a result of the different roles I had fulfilled.

In my first school I was offered the opportunity to step up to a pastoral role, as an Assistant Head of House, in a school where the pastoral system was House-based, rather than year group or section-based. When I look back, I think I learnt more in that role than in any other, until I became a Head. My Head of House and I had oversight of the progress and well-being of a quarter of the school. Siblings were placed in the same house, so we built relationships with families. I had to deal with safeguarding/child protection and discipline issues; take assemblies (initially terrifying, ultimately energising and stimulating!); manage primary liaison; communicate with external agencies and, of course, lead our tutor team. I grew considerably in confidence, resilience and expertise during my time in the role.

From there I moved to be second in department, then Head of Department, then Head of Sixth Form, Deputy Head and finally Headteacher. Leading the Sixth Form section was a brilliant balance of both pastoral and academic responsibility. I became a pastoral deputy – and the single deputy in a school of 1100 where, when the head was out of school, I stepped up. That was a varied, sometimes unpredictable, but hugely satisfying role. And after five years in that post, I moved to be a head, a position I held for ten years. I realised how much pastoral care (of staff and parents, in addition to pupils) the role involved. By this stage I felt well-placed to rise to the challenge.

So, my advice to you all is to build your experience, avoid being pigeon-holed and confined to one 'ladder', and have a wide-ranging, rewarding and joyful career! I hope you enjoy it as much as I enjoyed mine.

Questions to Ask of Yourself, Your Team, Your Staff, Your Students or Your Wider Community

Do I have experiences which translate into the field of pastoral care – can I articulate these and link them to predicted responsibilities within a pastoral role?

What experience do I have of managing behaviour, attendance, wellbeing, safeguarding, etc.?

- Does my school offer developmental opportunities linked to pastoral care – if not, can I suggest opportunities or even lead interventions/support?

- Does my school offer enough extra-curricular opportunities for students – could I offer some of my time to lead, or support with the leadership, of an activity?

- Does my school offer domain/subject specific training/CPD regularly and is pastoral care a feature of the school's CPD calendar?

- Am I active within communities which could further my professional development? Are these physical and located close to me? Do I capitalise on the wide range of experience/advice available through online social media?

- As a leader, am I aware of the motivations/goals that my staff have – am I aware of their past experiences and their ability to contribute to areas which may be outside of their current remit? Is there untapped experience going to waste in my school?

- As an aspiring member of pastoral staff, have I discussed my motivations/goals with my line manager or other appropriate staff?

- Have I visited other schools to see how they develop staff or to appraise myself of the developmental/CPD opportunities they offer?

- As a leader, do I reflect upon whether our vacancies are filled internally or externally and whether there is a balance i.e., do we develop enough of our own staff?

- If turnover is high for our pastoral teams do we conduct real, informative exit interviews which try to hone in on areas of concern?

 Finding/Securing Pastoral Care Roles

There is such a wide variety of pastoral roles available now within our education system, as we have already seen, due to the expansion of the pastoral care sector. Generally, the processes for seeking and securing roles however, will be very similar. Many of the roles we advertise in pastoral care utilise similar sets of skills, depend upon shared knowledge and require particular attitudes. In this chapter, you will find a myriad of advice and support for securing the right pastoral role for you ranging from finding the information you need about the school all the way through to those tricky final, formal interview questions.

Initial Considerations

As part of your research, you should be visiting, or calling, any school with a role you are interested in. For a pastoral role you want to speak to the person in charge of pastoral care – this sounds obvious but sometimes you may not be offered this opportunity so I would encourage you to follow up with an email, addressed to this person, if you have further questions that weren't answered. Ultimately, they, along with the Headteacher, set the vision for pastoral care in the school and checking their values align with your own is key.

You then need to find out if the wider school system aligns with your vision for pastoral care. How will you feel if you apply for the job you've been wanting so desperately, only to find that the school's behaviour system makes you uncomfortable? What if you start the job and they tell you that for 15 hours a week you are the member of staff on-duty, alongside your other responsibilities?

All schools must publish key policies on their website – have a read of the behaviour policy, safeguarding, attendance, etc. and when you visit see if this is enacted. I have listed below a range of questions that any pastoral leader should be able to answer confidently when it comes to the school's systems, and that should give you a keen understanding of their approaches.

- *What are the key priorities for whoever is the successful candidate?*
- *What does a typical day look like in the role?*
- *What whole-school responsibilities are a part of the role?*
- *What is behaviour like in the school? What is behaviour like in classrooms?*
- *What are the biggest challenges for the pastoral team?*
- *What are the key points of the behaviour system?*
- *Are there any line management responsibilities or staff supporting the role?*
- *How are rewards utilised within the school?*
- *What strategies does the school use to improve attendance/punctuality?*
- *How are parents involved in the pastoral care of their children?*
- *How are SEND/EAL students supported in the school?*
- *How do you promote positive wellbeing/mental health within the school?*
- *What systems are in place to prevent, and educate around, bullying in the school?*
- *What systems are in place to support students from LGBTQ+ backgrounds?*
- *What methods/sources of alternative provision are in use at the school?*
- *What are the exclusion figures for this year – are these increasing or decreasing? What are most exclusions for?*
- *What is the experience of the pastoral team – how long have other staff been in post?*
- *How important is extra-curricular provision at the school and what kinds of activities are offered?*
- *How are tutors organised? What does the tutor time schedule look like?*

There are clearly many more potential questions that you could ask, and lots will depend upon context, but this gives you a starting point. If you get answers to those questions, you should be able to make a clear judgement about whether the school's pastoral system aligns closely with your own values and ethos. It's also then worth checking what you have heard against what you can find online about the school – use the government's data dashboard for schools to see their attendance figures, for example, and see that you have been given accurate information.

On any visit to the school before making an application, it is preferable for you to see the school during the day, wherever possible, to see it in action. Some schools will give specific dates/times for group tours/information events and others will offer individual tours at a time suitable for you. The latter is my preference and if you have the option to secure an individual tour, you should do so. Not only does this mean that you can move at a better pace and ask questions of the person conducting the tour in a much more controlled manner, but this also offers you a great opportunity to leave a lasting impression by asking all of the right questions.

If you do manage to secure the best tour possible (individual and during the school day) I'd also try and book it in for a time that crosses their lessons with some unstructured time – in an ideal world you want to see student behaviour in classrooms and at a break/lunch/after school. This will give you the best possible insight into the culture of the school – you should avoid tours, if possible, that happen at the end of the day and show you an empty building.

The Intricacies of Applying for a Pastoral Role

Once you have visited/discussed the role, you have the decision to make about whether to start the application process – not an enviable one as school application processes are all very similar and very different at the same time. It's tough to write about the application process in detail largely due to the fact most schools use different proformas and application methods. They all do follow similar conventions, though, in expecting you to respond to a person specification and write a cover letter or statement, with perhaps some sort of prompt or direction for your letter. If they do offer this extra guidance, it will likely focus on your experience of pastoral care, or vision for it.

It's important for you to have done your research into the school prior to any application and, alongside asking great questions during a tour/discussion, you should have looked at the school website and any social media. I always like to read the last few letters and newsletters, if available, to try and get a feeling for what is currently happening in the context of the school. Equally, put the feelers out to anybody in your network to find out more about the school, whether that is through your personal or online networks – Twitter/X is great for this and I can't overstate how many contacts I have made which have helped to gather information about roles/schools.

You should be able to pull all of this together, with your skills and experience, and articulate why you are a suitable candidate for the role you are applying for. The best letters will have a focus throughout on why you are not just a suitable candidate for the role but what you have learned about the school and why it is right for you. The longer I have worked in schools, the more importance I have placed on finding the right environment for me – aligning your vision and values with the culture of the school is of significant importance in ensuring you can make a sustainable impact and enjoy what you do.

I'd encourage you to ask somebody who knows you well to read your letter alongside somebody who knows you in a more professional capacity. Your letter and supporting evidence should capture 'you' and feel both honest and representative of who you are. Make sure you back up any statements you make with evidence of how you achieved them, what was the impact? How did you go about introducing it? What was key? How did your leadership affect it? Facts and figures will help here – if you can point to a % rise or a # drop etc. If you are trying to evidence something more abstract – how do you know it was successful? How did you measure and monitor it? You want to show the person reading that you are both reflective and strategic. A word on Artificial Intelligence - as tempting as it may be I would stay away from using AI to create your cover letter - as good as these tools currently are, their writing style is fairly easy to spot, and the last impression you wish to leave on recruiters is that you didn't take the time to engage with the process.

So, You Made The Shortlist!

Once you have completed and submitted your application, you must face the dreaded wait to find out if you have been shortlisted. If you are fortunate enough to have secured an interview, the likelihood is that your interview will be a one or half-day affair but, dependent upon the pastoral role, these may be shorter or longer. Most schools, depending on the number of applicants, will conduct a cut at lunchtime during a full-day interview process before taking a smaller number of candidates through to formal interviews. The tasks and interviews before this are there to demonstrate your suitability for the role, get a feel for you as a person/professional and see if you can back up what you wrote in your application.

There are a multitude of tasks/activities that I've come up against as an interviewee, and overseen as an interviewer, that feature here and the list, although not exhaustive, will likely be representative of any pastoral interviews.

The Tour

You should hopefully have been on a tour of the school prior to your application. Don't make the mistake of thinking this is a repeat or an opportunity to relax. The tour is as much of an interview activity as the other parts of the day. I believe the tour is a good opportunity for you to ask more 'personal' questions about the school and, most importantly, delve into what the students think, as they will often be the ones guiding you. It's tempting to blurt out any question you can think of to try and get the students on side and espousing how personable you were during the tour when they are asked to feedback, but I'd recommend being more pragmatic. I always found it beneficial to get them thinking by asking them to take you to the place they are most proud of in the school or point out areas that students have had a hand in developing or areas they feel need to be improved.

Tours become more problematic when there are multiple candidates being toured around. I've seen as many as six candidates to two students and that environment is one where people tend to start climbing over each other for some interaction with the students. It's not great and all I would recommend is that you ask some pointed questions but don't feel pressure to compete.

There is also the option of a tour conducted by staff rather than by students. Most of the same advice applies – just remember that staff opinions of you may hold a bit more sway during feedback!

The Data Task

A data task features often in pastoral interviews because you need to be comfortable presenting and interrogating data, whether that be linked to behaviour/achievement/attendance or academic performance. Tasks will very often focus on these areas – I've had everything from a single page of data to reams of paper to draw conclusions from. If you've done your research beforehand, there will probably be things you are already aware of that you can look out for immediately – perhaps exclusions are high, attendance too low or rewards well outweighed by sanctions. Your job will be to identify these and, in most cases, come up with some sort of action plan to address your biggest concerns.

If you can identify groups from this data that will put you in good stead – attendance might be an issue in the school, for example, but if this is negatively impacted mostly by boys then your response should factor this in. I'd encourage you to familiarise yourself with an action plan proforma – there are probably a number used in your current school, but Google is also your friend here. It will take the pressure off of trying to think about how you present an action plan, key performance indicators etc. in the moment, if you haven't done this before, and save you from scrawling frantically all over the paper!

The In-Tray

Generally, an In-Tray of some kind will feature during the process – a list of scenarios occurring in school, with some safeguarding issues thrown in, that you must prioritise and often justify why. As long as you identify the safeguarding issues, and place them at the top, the justifications thereafter will be largely down to opinion. There are generally two models of how this information is then used – some schools will take away your sheet and the panel will evaluate your responses. The other option is that you will be asked to keep hold of the sheet and you will be asked to talk through your decision-making process during the formal interview.

What order would you prioritise the following scenarios?

It's the middle of the school day:

1. A call has just come in to reception that students in your year group were throwing stones into traffic after school yesterday.
2. A student is waiting outside of your office in tears.
3. You've received a duty call to attend a science classroom on the other side of the school. You haven't got any further information.
4. You have a deadline of this afternoon to submit your governors' report to the Head of Key Stage.
5. A member of staff has emailed you to say a student has just disclosed, in her lesson, that she has been self-harming.
6. You are delivering an assembly in the morning and you haven't started planning it yet.

Is there a right answer? Not really. There is a key safeguarding issue on here which is #5 and this must take immediate priority. There are then two admin issues, the assembly and the governors' report, which I would expect to see at the bottom of your list. The three 'live' issues of the call to reception, the student in tears and the duty call all require a fairly speedy response. Personally, I would take account of the context given at the start of the task, that it is the middle of the school day, and use this as justification to leave resolving the students who have been throwing stones until later in the day. This then gives you the duty call and the student in tears to deal with – the biggest issue is the duty call – at this point, we don't know what this is for. It could be that a student needs to go to the toilet or that they've collapsed and so this has to take priority.

There is room here for justification and interviewers will be accepting of you using your research here i.e., part of your justification for dealing with the student in tears after could be that you know that the Head of Year and Assistant Head of Year share an office and you could ask them to pick this issue up.

As stated above, as long as you have clearly identified the most pressing safeguarding concern, this is the biggest hurdle for representing yourself well on this task – but do bear in mind that there can often be more than one. I attended an interview once with five things to prioritise – all of which were safeguarding concerns and that definitely took a little longer to prioritise – ultimately it was about looking into which of them had the most immediate and pressing risk of danger to staff/students and then working backwards from there.

The Letter

You are given a topic and asked to write a letter to a parent, or sometimes another stakeholder, regarding an issue you have been presented with. This could be anything from an issue in a lesson or subject to a student being bullied. Ensure your letter is clear and concise and addresses the points raised. Don't make any promises other than to investigate and to get back to the person – I always like to state a date for when I will respond and add that I will make contact, even if there is no resolution, so that the parent can be kept up to date.

As part of this task, you may also be asked to follow-up with an action plan of what you would do next after writing the letter. Again, if producing/writing letters for a given audience is something you aren't familiar with, or don't have experience of, take a look at some of the recent letters sent out on the school's website and try to develop an understanding for how they communicate.

If the school you are applying to serves a community where there are a large number of English as an Additional Language students, I'd be willing to wager that their letters are very clear and concise for the purposes of translation or simplicity. Writing a wordy, academic letter as part of your interview task at a school like this may well show you have misjudged your audience.

The Group Discussion or 'Goldfish Bowl'

Welcome to hell. If there's a task on an interview day I hate more than any other it's the Goldfish Bowl. A simulated group discussion on a topic, or range of topics, in which you are supposed to discuss and keep the conversation going and on task. You may be assigned a role if the interviewers particularly hate you. I believe that this task is out of date and is a poor attempt to replicate the realities of a meeting with multiple attendees but there are some holdouts in school leadership who think this is an effective recruitment tool.

My advice for this task is to be yourself and contribute where you feel you can. If there is one thing that this task does achieve it's that it shows an observer who you wouldn't want on your team. The person clambering to interject at every opportunity or shouting over others to have their point heard. Try to make clear and concise points and build upon the contributions made by others – if you disagree with a point made then do so politely and with sound reasoning. One other good tip is to use people's names when you are talking to them – it sounds common sense but when you are presented with a table of, effectively strangers, and you are competing for a role it can be easy to forget the more 'human' norms of an actual conversation! Finally, remember that good leaders bring ideas out of others - if you spot someone is quiet or being spoken over, take the opportunity to say "X, is there anything you'd add to the conversation?" to show you are aware of others.

There is no 'how-to' guide on how to do well in a Goldish Bowl as it is so subjective – I have been given feedback after one such activity that responding first, if there is silence, shows that you are willing to put yourself on the line to start the ball rolling. I've also been given feedback to never contribute first and to always wait for somebody else to offer their point so that you can build upon what they've said. The reality is that actual meetings don't work like this – take any feedback after a Goldfish Bowl with a pinch of salt.

The Group Task

You may also face any other range of group tasks – these could have a focus, like the discussions previously, or you may be tasked with achieving something as a group. At an interview for a Head of House role, I was part of a group in which we had to design a transition plan for Year 6 pupils coming up to the school. Again, the same advice follows – be yourself, be honest and contribute where you can.

The Role Play

I've only ever experienced two role-plays – one was a telephone conversation with a 'parent', played by the Deputy Head, ringing in to discuss a staff member racially abusing a pupil. The other was a conversation with a 'parent' about the progress of their child in a mock progress meeting. If you are put into a role-play scenario acknowledge in your head that it is strange but treat it as if was a formal interview. This is another area where your prior research will benefit you – you might be able to refer to the school's behaviour system or safeguarding policy to back up your points and shut down avenues for the role-player to go down. If you are at the point of an interview it's because you have the skills and experience and have probably done this day-to-day. Don't let the awkwardness of the situation throw you off.

The Presentation

Presentations can cover anything but will likely have some sort of link to the role, your own vision and values or wider school life. As with any presentation, make sure that it is clear and concise, that you have timed and rehearsed it well and that you have run through it with somebody else. This will help you to anticipate any follow-up questions which you will be able to deftly answer! Do some simple things to show you know the school – add their logo, user their colours or feature their motto, etc. Wherever you can you should also use the opportunity to present more of yourself – if the presentation is on how you would improve behaviour at John Smith Academy, they aren't looking for it to be just based on research or best practice, the panel want to hear how you've translated these things into reality. Begin with the research or what you know, absolutely, but follow up with how you've achieved those things in your practice and what the impact has been. Anyone can research a presentation topic – ensure that you use the time wisely to share exactly why you'd be great for the job at hand.

The Assembly

I think delivering an assembly to a room of students and staff you don't know is one of the hardest tasks you can be given for any role, whether you are experienced in delivering assemblies or not, but the same principles apply as your presentation. If you can I'd encourage you to welcome students into the hall/space as they enter, but these situations may be managed for you. If the person introducing you doesn't say who you are and why you are there, then do this yourself. Most kids will be on board when they hear you are there for an interview and will feel that they have been trusted with this information.

This might be another opportunity to include some of your research – say you are given the topic of 'the benefits of reading' and it says on the school website that students have a tutor time session each week dedicated to reading, mention it. You will be continuing to show those observing you that you have tried to develop an understanding of the school and its context.

Try to get some audience participation by taking students hands up to answer a question or make a comment – if you are particularly nervous or it's your first time doing this then control this even more 'Okay, somebody from the front row, can you tell me..' – this will open you up to less opportunities for disruption in an unfamiliar environment. When you finish the assembly, make sure to thank the students for listening.

The Student Activity

These can be incredibly varied, but I'd also suggest they aren't very common. In one scenario, I had to deliver a talk about an object that was meaningful to me with a small class, in another the students from the school council had been tasked with making a decision and my role was to facilitate this. I have used tasks such as 'create a poster for an anti-bullying non-uniform day' with a candidate assigned to support a group of 2–4 students to see how they interact with the children assigned. Make sure to introduce yourself, try to use their names and bring them onboard for anything you do/discuss. The observers will be looking for how you engage with the students and whether you are capable of building relationships in the short time you have with them.

The Speed Date

You may find yourself in a room, rotating through conversations with a range of staff, designed to give multiple people the chance to question and get a feel for you – or the opposite and you will be given the chance to question them. I would recommend using this opportunity to find out about the people you may be working with, rather than the school.

You will have a very short amount of time to have these discussions and focusing on the staff you might be working with is a good strategy to find out whether the school is right for you. Ask them whether they receive regular CPD/line management? Are they supported in their roles? What's their favourite thing about working at the school? How long have they been there? I really like this as an activity and have only seen it rarely – it gives candidates the opportunity to do the thing most important on interview days which is to meet, and talk to, staff.

The Student Panel

I've found student panels to be ever-present on pastoral interview days. Don't fall into the trap of thinking this is the 'If you were a biscuit what would you be?' panel as often students will be asking some hard-hitting questions. That's not to say the 'softer' question interview panels don't exist – I have attended an interview where 10 out 12 questions on the student panel were in the vein of 'What Avenger would you be if given the choice?" – this tells me as a candidate that the school either haven't planned well with the students or don't think that they can be trusted to ask real questions.

With the student panels you will need to be able to tailor your responses to your audience. The same advice applies here as I suggested for any task involving students – make sure you introduce yourself and try to remember their names and use these when you give your responses or ask follow-up questions. In a pastoral role, they will want to see you show warmth and empathy but also demonstrate that you can lead and be firm. Use examples to back up your responses that will resonate with the students and that they will have understanding/experience of and try not to be as formal as you would in the final interview.

The Formal Interview

The final part of the day, if you make it through, will be the formal interview. I've tried below to collate a range of interview questions relevant to pastoral care – lots of these I have been asked before. Don't rehearse answers to the point they feel hollow – I don't tend to look at interview questions anymore but find being able to think about the issues they present or how my answers have changed is a useful exercise. You could have a list of 1000 questions and still be asked something new in an interview – it's more sensible, certainly from my perspective, to think about your experience and tailor them to different questions. Think of a time when you faced a really challenging behaviour from a student – how could you use that example and link it to a valid answer for the three questions below?

1. A pastoral leader must be comfortable dealing with challenging behaviour – can you give an example of when you have done this and how you resolved the situation?
2. What is the most important skill for a pastoral leader to have and why?
3. What do you believe is the purpose of pastoral care?

I worked with a challenging student who would not show up at any point in the day to show senior staff his report card – I offered him the chance to come to me, or breakfast club, in the mornings to grab something to eat. Every day, he showed up with his report card because that wasn't the reason he was coming to see me. I can translate that single experience into all three of the questions above – number 1 is fairly obvious, the student was refusing to follow the instructions of senior staff in the simple act of showing them his report card, never mind the behaviour he was on report for. I can also use this example in question two – I believe the most important skill for a pastoral leader to have is patience – here's an example of how I have demonstrated this. What is the purpose of Pastoral Care? To develop relationships/systems that enable students to access education in situations where they otherwise aren't – my example can then be built in to show that I had to think outside of the box to build a situation where this student engaged with the behaviour system, and thus allowed us to address his behaviour, enabling him to access education. Broadly speaking if you can make a point, provide some evidence and discuss the impact, you should be on the right lines for any answer you give.

Additional Questions to Consider:

What would be the first three things you would do, in the role, if you were successful today?

How would you use assessment to support progress and attainment in your key stage/year group?

How would you develop a shared vision/ethos within your year group?

How important is communication with parents/carers for a pastoral leader?

What does inclusion look like in a successful year group? How would you ensure that all students needs are met?

A pastoral leader must be comfortable dealing with challenging behaviour – can you give an example of when you have done this and how you resolved the situation?

How have you contributed to the development of the school community in your career so far?

How involved should a pastoral leader be in the development of teaching and learning?

Give an example of a situation where you have used rewards/praise to motivate a student.

What is the biggest issue currently facing pastoral staff in schools?

You have received a complaint from a parent that their child is being bullied – what do you do?

Can you share an occasion where an intervention or strategy you have been a part of has failed and what were your reflections?

How does play/unstructured time factor into the development of children and how do we ensure that we develop this?

How would you manage a diverse team of tutors at varying stages of their career?

You disagree with elements of the school's new behaviour policy – how do you deal with this?

What are you most looking forward to about potentially taking on this role?

One of your tutors is refusing to follow the tutor time schedule you have designed. How do you deal with this?

You will be line managing an Assistant Head of Year – how would you ensure you build a strong working relationship?

Give an example of an occasion where you have built a relationship with a challenging student.

A student has reported to you that a member of staff smells of alcohol – how do you respond?

You have heard a rumour that explicit pictures of a student are being shared around the school – what are your next steps?

> How would you handle a child disclosing something sensitive to you?
>
> How would you deal with a student making a bullying allegation against another?
>
> **Secondary Head of Year Specific:**
>
> Year 7 – How would you ensure an effective transition process from Year 6 to Year 7?
>
> Year 8/9 – What would be your primary focus to engage your year group with school life? What steps would you take to develop a positive attitude towards options choices in Year 9?
>
> Year 10 – How would you promote positive attitudes towards homework and the expectations of GCSEs?
>
> Year 11 – What role does a Head of Year play in supporting the Post-16 options process?

That covers some of the wide variety of the tasks you could be asked to undertake. There will clearly be some I have missed but these will be the core components of an interview and, if you prepare well for these, there won't be much that could surprise you. Pastoral interviews are trending towards being half-day to full-day affairs, with some even stretching into two days. My feeling is that this is too much and is an unnecessary drain on the time of the school and of the candidates involved – if you are recruiting, I'd encourage you to think about whether you can find out everything you need about candidates from shorter interview experiences which limit the amount of time for staff to be absent from their own schools.

Interviews in schools have become quite the behemoth over recent years – there aren't many other sectors like it in terms of the gauntlet that staff must run through as the seniority of the roles they are applying for increases – there are lessons for us to learn from those other sectors in ensuring that we aren't forcing candidates to run that gauntlet unnecessarily.

Handling Rejection

A final word – on those disappointing days where we aren't the successful candidate. Don't let it defeat you. Each school is different and on any given day they may be looking for something specific – if it doesn't work out for you then pick yourself up and get back on the horse. I can only write in such detail about interview days because I've done so many – I haven't been successful at all of them, and I'd wager I've been unsuccessful more than successful at this point. It's no reflection on me or my ability to do the job I applied for, just as it isn't on you. Take onboard any useful feedback given (this isn't always forthcoming, and feedback can often be the most frustrating part of the day) and then dust yourself off and start again.

During your recruitment preparation, you will have seen pastoral leaders/staff dealing with some of the most extreme incidents in the school. You may also have heard them discuss the awful issues they have to deal with around safeguarding or social care, for example, and the lasting impression these things often have on them. It's safe to say school-based pastoral care has become a sometimes-untamable beast with the stripping back of many public services – as soon as you think you've reached the last email, in comes another.

Yet pastoral care is a field which consistently draws great people into it – ultimately, education is a caring profession and pastoral care requires the most caring of us all. You are going to come up against great people at all stages of your pastoral care recruitment journey and, as much as that can be frustrating, it's equally a wonderful thing for our children that so many good people want to take on these demanding, draining but absolutely delightful roles. Don't be disheartened if you don't get the one you want the first time.

Questions to Ask of Yourself, Your Team, Your Staff, Your Students or Your Wider Community

- What are the questions I would struggle to answer the most, if asked, at interview and how can I develop my knowledge and experience in these areas?
- What are the tasks I would struggle to complete, if given them during interview, and how can I develop my knowledge and skills in these areas?
- Am I clear on why I am applying to a particular school/what appeals to me about the role I am applying for?
- What are they key behaviours/attributes I would expect to display as a member of a pastoral team?
- Do I have any skills that the school have noted are missing within their current pastoral team? For example, Mental Health First Aid, Coaching, etc.

Have I met/spoken to different members of this school community – can I see myself as a part of it?

After an interview day – did I get a good 'vibe' from the school; the students and the community. Can I see myself working here? It can be tempting to accept a role because you've put the time into interviewing and applying for it – if it doesn't feel right… don't make the mistake!

5 Leading Staff

As a member of the pastoral team, you will very regularly be given the opportunity to lead staff as the expert on a particular student, area, group, etc. This brings with it many opportunities to develop yourself but also to develop the staff around you. Depending on the context of your school and the way that the pastoral staff/roles are structured, you may find yourself being the most senior person available to respond to an issue/incident or the expert in the room on a child who is really struggling. Staff will look to you for advice, guidance and support on many things and you need to be comfortable in this field. For some, leadership comes naturally and standing in front of a hall full of staff delivering CPD or storming into the middle of an incident and taking charge is second nature – for others this is developed over time through skill/experience. Developing your ability to lead is multi-faceted as there is no one-size-fits-all methodology for leading people – particularly in a profession as varied as schools.

In this chapter, I cover the great responsibility that comes with leading staff in schools in two sections – focusing on leading staff in general and then a wider discussion on the key pastoral leadership of tutor/key stage staff. When most of us enter the education sector to lead young people, with a particular focus on how to get the best out of the teams you lead. Whether you are leading pastoral staff, tutors or engaging with staff adjacent to, or above, you this chapter brings together a range of practical support for leading with clarity and purpose through discussion of leadership styles, strategies and specific advice to succeed.

Section 1 – All Staff

Evolving Styles of Leadership

There is a change occurring within line-management that will, I believe, soon be commonplace within schools in which a coaching model is advocated for the line-management of staff – the crux of which is listening and asking the right questions to ensure that people develop, followed up with modelling and observing the intended practise. This is a model that has always served me well in leading staff – ultimately, we all want to be listened to and feel that our opinions have been heard. It's cliched but the old 'Teach a man to fish' quote serves us well here – as a line manager I can respond to my staff members' concerns by doing the job for them, or providing the answer, but in reality that will provide a level of dependency that a good leader will be trying to move away from.

Ask questions, help your staff to understand why they've made a decision; how that decision might impact themselves and others; how it will drive, or not drive, school/faculty improvement, etc. The end result may be that they are more assured of their decision than before or it may that you've teased out thinking from them, which has made them reconsider or explore a different approach – either way you are contributing to the development of a reflective leader.

Responding To Concerns Big or Small

Through your role, you will be exposed to a wide variety of different behaviours exhibited by students, staff and stakeholders. These may be things you've never had to deal with personally, that are extreme or perhaps the opposite and, in your eyes, trivial. I always followed the mantra that if somebody raises a concern with me, no matter how or big or small, it deserves to be followed up. You may not be able to do so immediately, but that person felt they needed support - whatever the issue may be you can either do something to address it yourself or help them devise strategies so that they can fix it themselves.

I remember early in my career being called to a classroom 'on-call' as a member of staff was struggling with his group. I was standing in a busy office as the call came through and it was fairly specific in what he was struggling with – a student at the back of the room kept tapping a pencil. This drew a fairly negative response from a couple of members of staff in earshot who said he shouldn't be calling 'on-call' for something so stupid – but to him it wasn't and, in reality, is a highly disruptive behaviour. It was disrupting his lesson and he couldn't find a way to solve the problem – he needed someone to listen to him and help him. This was an opportunity to support, rather than criticise, and I remember going back at the end of the day to see if there was any more that we could do. To say he was grateful for the support would be the understatement of the century.

You will also be exposed to things you find devastating, hilarious, annoying, tiring and much more – remember that you aren't alone in your role. You are part of a pastoral team and, particularly while you are new to the role, you should access support as you need it. Leadership very rarely occurs in isolation and you would be foolish not to capitalise on the leadership capacity available within your teams.

Communication is Key

As well as listening to staff being a huge part of leading them, so is communication, whether this is with staff you directly lead/line manage or on a larger scale/whole school level. There are clearly going to be things you cannot share with people for any number of reasons; safeguarding, confidentiality or even the fact it's something you know they will react poorly to. The vast majority of the time, however we should aim to be open and honest with staff as we navigate the world of pastoral care. If you have been in a pastoral care role you will be well accustomed to a conversation with a member of staff where you are discussing a student and they are reeling off all of the issues they have with them – you then throw in a piece of vital information that explains some of the reasons behind this and their face drops. They say "Oh, if I'd known that I might have been able to come at the problem in a different way" and you curse yourself for not sharing the information in the first place. What about when you overheard a conversation between two members of staff who are discussing the fact that Ahmed never gets sanctions and he's always getting away with his misbehaviour – except you remember quite clearly the 2 hours of detentions he sat with you the day before.

Our lives as pastoral staff are made much easier when we involve staff and make it clear to them the outcomes of something we have dealt with – it's often hard in a busy environment but the impact of not doing this on your culture can be catastrophic. I still have to push myself to do this on occasion and not assume that something that's obvious to me is obvious to the wider staff team! One of the biggest cultural destabilisers in a school is a perception from staff that behaviour issues are not dealt with, or are swept under the rug, and it's an easy fix to ensure that we communicate with individual staff where we have intervened on their behalf or with the wider staff body when students have received larger or more significant sanctions. Conversely, it's important to ensure that we share student success far and wide and that this is heard and received by staff – one of the best places to do this is during assemblies.

Our assembly calendar is important as it is an opportunity to share key cultural messages or communicate what is important to us as pastoral/school leaders. Think about who you want to be in assemblies hearing these messages – very often in secondary schools' assemblies are only attended by the tutor team and pastoral leaders with a member of SLT supporting/leading. In primary schools, there is the opportunity to deliver whole school assemblies and ensure consistency of message, which is a hugely valuable tool. Consider this further, though – do you ensure that all staff in the school whether they are admin, teaching assistants or IT technicians attend assemblies? If the messages we are sharing are so culturally valuable to our school, then surely everyone in them should see the week's assembly at least once, allowing us to further propagate and disseminate our key messaging.

Communication is a Two-Way Street

With communication being vaunted as key it is important to emphasise that this is a two-way street. There are so many opportunities to work with teaching and support staff to develop our knowledge of strategies that work for students within our area of responsibility. Sometimes we can get so caught up in the all-consuming eater-of-days that is pastoral care that it's hard to step back and look at what's working within small microcosms of the school. That group of girls that hate each other and would quite happily push each other off of a cliff and into a gathering group of sharks? They are all engaged and doing great in Maths. Why? Spend some time investigating by observing the class. We need to be able to spot where there are areas of success and disseminate this into the wider school. Not only does this save us time as pastoral staff but it also opens doors to bring staff further into pastoral life and develop that culture of understanding that stops us being cursed under people's breath as the disruptors of lessons.

Part of this also necessitates an engagement with faculty-level data – if you aren't looking at behaviour, achievement data, etc. for specific faculties for the students you work with – why not? You should be able to make comparisons and spot trends, identify hotspots for poor behaviour or areas where it's alarmingly quiet for Cole from 8DG. Interacting with faculty data also allows you to open up those conversations with teaching staff that you may not have had otherwise. One of our Maths teachers was having a nightmare with a student and, teaching him four times a week, was becoming something he dreaded. What became clear through conversation was that he taught him three times straight after lunch and once in the morning. The student has ADHD and, through conversation with his parents and their subsequent visit to his ADHD nurse, he moved to trialing a dose of his medication in the middle of the day, which had a dramatic impact for those Maths lessons. This may not have been spotted without opening this channel of communication with his Maths teacher, as it could have just been assumed that he wasn't behaving in Maths – the reality being that 3 hours of his time after lunch each week was spent in a situation where his medication had effectively worn off.

By opening doors and channels for communication with staff, we develop our presence as members of pastoral staff, or as a wider pastoral team, which further facilitates increased communication at a variety of levels. One of our goals as pastoral staff should be to share the incredibly useful knowledge that we have developed about students, that teaching staff may not be exposed to regularly. If we want to develop a culture of understanding around the pastoral needs of the school community, we can't keep this information to ourselves and we need to vary our approaches to disseminating it. We always have opportunities to share best practise when it comes to Teaching and Learning – how often do we do this for pastoral care? How many opportunities do you create for staff to discuss strategies that work with particular students, to collaborate on things that work and strategise on how to improve those that don't? Part of minimising any battle between pastoral and teaching needs is in building mutual understanding – visibility is key in this.

Section 2: Leading a Team of Tutors

I have split this chapter into two sections deliberately – often a key focus of pastoral staff/leaders is on getting tutor/key stage teams functioning at a high level. If you are responsible for a tutor team, or key stage team in primary, then you need them to have your back – they may take isolated/misbehaving pupils for you, cover the team briefing or plan a tutor time activity. They will be the ones who see each and every one of their group, every day. They will be the ones, on the ground, helping to turn vision into reality and backing up the pastoral needs of the school as the first line of defence. This section will likely be most beneficial for secondary pastoral staff but I hope there may be some areas that provide useful information for primary/FE colleagues also.

First and foremost, you need to focus on supporting your team and continuing the trend of being visible, visit tutor time sessions, ensure that any tutor time work/activities are resourced and ready to go for them. I think tutors, and the time that they have with their tutees, is of huge importance to the culture of a year group and by extension, the school. Many schools have moved towards, or are moving towards, tutor time being an extension of other lessons (English catch-up, numeracy sessions, etc.) and I think this underappreciates the value a tutor holds to their tutees. If you can provide opportunities for your tutors to just be with their tutor group, getting to know them, supporting them, re-enforcing year group/whole school messages then do it – you'll see and feel the impact.

We are often bound by the structures/demands placed upon us but finding opportunities to develop your year/key stage culture is important – I always run a Friday Tutor Quiz using an online quiz platform and we award a trophy each week to the winning form. It's silly and often gets a bit loud but fundamentally it brings everyone together and we have some shared competition – it's also a great opportunity to push cultural events or areas you want to develop some knowledge in your students. I had some feedback from a parent that they would like us to run an assembly on Autism to help her child's peer group understand their needs/difficulties – I ended up asking them to create me a quiz focusing on autism which was a hit with students and engaged them more than any assembly could have.

As a Head of Year/Pastoral Leader your tutor team(s) are the backbone of the pastoral care system for your year group. You can't see every student, every day, but they sure do. Most schools will stress that a child's tutor is a parent's first port of call and the person their child should take any concerns to when they initially arise and so ensuring they are as strong and motivated as possible can be key to the success of your role. A strong tutor team is confident, supportive and challenging – whether that is with their tutees, yourself or the parents they liaise with. The best tutors care deeply about their tutees and establish warm relationships built on high expectations whilst balancing the ability to be that go-to person at any given time. So, how do we go about building a brilliant tutor team?

Support/Development

Part of your role as a middle leader is to develop those around you and to ensure that the staff who are working with you have opportunities to grow. As a pastoral leader, the likelihood is you won't have any official line management responsibility for your tutors, or the teachers within your key stage, and so it would be easy to abdicate responsibility for developing them, but I feel that you must dedicate time to this. It's usually the case that a tutor team will include members of staff at a wide variety of career levels – some who have been in their role for the last 30 years and some who are stepping into their NQT year – that doesn't however make it any easier to identify those opportunities for development as it might with classroom teaching.

The role of a tutor is both challenging and rewarding as you see your tutees fail, flourish and eventually fly away from you and during that time the opportunities you can afford your tutors for development are varied. Some initial questions to think about around that development are below:

- Do you have a tutor that is new to the profession and is looking for the opportunity to plan and produce a set of tutor time activities to have a wider whole-school impact?
- Do you have a tutor looking to work in pastoral care or take on a more active role in whole school behaviour/achievement? Could they take students onto report or devise a tutor or year group achievement program/activity?
- Do you have a tutor looking to expand their proficiency with data? Could they produce a tracker for key information for other tutors, that is, a weekly behaviour points/attendance/achievement/punctuality table for the year group?
- Do you have a tutor looking to build their confidence? Could they lead a year group assembly with or without their tutor group?
- Do you have a tutor with an untapped skill set? Perhaps a hobby or area of interest that they could use within your year team or a particular group of students?
- Do you have a tutor that is struggling with managing their tutor group or getting the best from them? Could they be paired up with an experienced tutor in the team to observe some tutor times for the benefit of both tutors?

There are many ways for you to develop your tutors and your wider tutor team and the stronger they are, the stronger you are. It pays to develop those around you, and it is certainly an area to reflect on.

Case Study 5.1 The Power of a Good Tutor by Ceri Stokes – Assistant Principal for Safeguarding

'Targets, actions and evidence', or some variant of this, is a phrase that comes up again and again for me in my role as a safeguarding leader. As teachers we are used to academic targets but from a pastoral point of view, this can be challenging, especially when the target is to make friends or to be happy. What actions can we take as a school and how can you measure and evidence this?

Those that are used to dealing with Mental Health issues will be aware of tools like the SDQ (Strengths and Difficulties Questionnaires) or the jellybean man tree for younger students but in my experience these can be challenging for some students and staff to use as a communication tool; to interpret effectively and don't always bring clear actions. They do however give you a good base of evidence to build strategies from. What I have found to work are activities that create opportunities for reflection for either the students or staff involved. When we look at a strategy or intervention and see that it isn't working – what can we do? Here are two examples:

A pupil was struggling with the idea of 'being happy'. Their tutor suggested that they come and talk to him every week to off load. It seemed a good action and one that could be evidenced. However, the child came every week and offloaded all the time, even when the issue was small compared to initial concerns raised. It almost felt like they had to have a problem and that was the only way the child knew how to talk or share - they were never discussing the positive things - and there were many. The tutor felt that nothing was being achieved, and if anything he noticed that it was removing the child from their friend group. So he decided to do a wellbeing chart for his whole tutor group, where they emailed him an emoji of how they were feeling, but kept it in a chart form so they can see how the week and month was going. The child saw that it was ok to talk about positive things even when things were bad at home and that they shouldn't feel guilty for being happy – the idea that other students were able to experience positive and negative feelings at once was powerful for him. The tutor was still available should the child need him, but slowly over time this became less of an issue and the tutor would bump into the student having fun at break with friends. Although the action changed, the target and evidence was achieved by a tutor who took an interest in a student and their mental health/wellbeing and used a novel idea to help them frame and understand their emotions.

In another example a child who was a Young Carer had a suggested target which was to attend a club with other Young Carers, so that they could connect and support each other. This child did not like this target and kept 'forgetting' to attend but would then be found on their own at lunch and break and often talked

> about how alone they felt. They didn't want others to know about their family situation and hated the idea that they were different but didn't know how to make friends. Their linked tutor came up with an idea for a "games club" and invited a few select people from the year group, some who were lonely, some who were quiet but a mix of different individuals. They played board games like Cluedo, and quickly this became the thing those students looked forward to. The initial idea of an individual level of support again was adapted by a tutor who spotted that a intervention wasn't working and then used their initiative to bring students to the child rather than to try and get the child to initiate these interactions themselves.

Be Accepting of Challenge

As a governor I've always liked the term 'critical friend' when used to describe the relationship between Headteacher and governors and I think this is also a good relationship to try and foster within your tutor team. Being a tutor can be an emotion filled role and it is sometimes the case that those emotions can spill over into frustration – having worked in a challenging school where tutor team briefings could often become a barrage of questions on "What's happening about this student?" or "Why is X still doing this?" you should aim to foster a culture where challenging questions can be asked of you in an appropriate way, at an appropriate time.

Challenge from tutors about what is happening within the year group is good, if only to keep you on your toes, and part of building a team that trusts your decision making and strategy is being able to respond adequately to that challenge. Your tutors need to know that they can bring you a problem and that you will either do your utmost to address it or that you will be able to give them an explanation for why that problem can't be solved in the way they desire. Feel confident in saying that you don't have an answer to a question and need to go away and think about it, or that it isn't the best time to ask. Tell them that you will speak to them in x amount of time whether you have an answer or not so that they know they aren't being fobbed off.

Well-Planned Tutor Activities

Tutor time in schools has seen an overhaul in recent years and most schools will use the time to complete a myriad of activities, whether that's literacy and numeracy sessions, silent reading, quizzes, uniform/equipment checks, sharing of topical information or a variety of other tasks based around school priorities. There is nothing more frustrating as a tutor than being instructed to do any of these things and not receiving the support or resources needed to undertake them. If you are expecting your tutors to run a topical news quiz every Friday, for example, then provide them with the resources to do so – whether that means sourcing it yourself or, as stated earlier, finding somebody willing to do so from a developmental perspective. Not only will this make your tutors feel supported, but it will give you the ability to standardise and monitor what is occurring within tutor time – if eight different tutors are running eight different quizzes, how can you know whether what is happening is having the effect you desired?

Equally if you are instructing tutors to perform checks on areas such as uniform/equipment then you should ensure that you circulate during these when you can – no tutor wants to feel isolated in this process and having your support once in a while will do wonders for their ability to enforce the rules that you, or the school, have set when you aren't there. Don't leave them to fight against the world on their own.

If you ask your tutors to analyse their tutees data checking attendance, etc. then make sure that they know how to do this in the least amount of time through training, or better yet, provide them with the data. I hate seeing staff labouring over tasks that could be done in a matter of minutes because they've been asked to do something but haven't been instructed on how to do it in the most efficient way. Again, this will help to ensure that standards are met within your team too and that tutors have no reason not to undertake the activities that you are asking of them.

Well-Planned Tutor Meetings

Another area to ensure that you plan well is your tutor team meetings or briefings. You will likely have a slot during the week to meet with your tutors and disseminate any important messages and catch up with how the team is doing as a group. Treat this time like you would any other meeting within the school and provide tutors with an agenda in advance of the meeting and ask for them to notify you of any other business at the end – ensuring there is adequate time to discuss this at the end. Staff time is at a premium and there is nothing worse than attending meetings that don't hold value just because they are on the calendar.

Consider the Questions Below

What information do you share/discuss at tutor team briefings? Are they for you to share information or for you to receive information?

Are your meetings well planned with an agenda prepared in advance and disseminated in time for tutors to reflect on it?

Is there a clear structure in your meetings or are issues raised as people think of them? It's frustrating to be sat in a meeting where one tutor is discussing an issue in their tutor group or with a tutee as if it was a one-to-one conversation. This is not the time for those kinds of conversations unless there is an application to the whole year group or other tutors.

Is there a better way to disseminate some of the information you currently share in tutor team briefings?

If you are allowing tutors to suggest AOB items – do you consider their merit/worth to the meeting at hand before adding them?

If a tutor misses your briefings/meetings – would it have any impact on them? If so, do you need to re-evaluate the core content/purpose?

Share Key Information

You are a team. As the Head of Year for that team you have access to a significant amount of privileged and useful information – some of which you can, and should, disseminate to your tutors to ensure that they can support you and the children in their tutor groups. If you are taking on a new year group/tutor team, this also works in reverse and they will have lots of information about their tutees that you should tap into.

Whenever you receive a piece of information about a child that could impact their time at school you should decide whether this would be useful for their tutor to know. There are clearly many things that need to be kept confidential and in the strictest confidence, but this is for you to judge as a professional – as stated before – your tutors are the ones who see these students every day and so are in the best position to notice changes in them. If you are sharing information that is of a sensitive or potentially upsetting nature, be aware also of the impact it could have on the individual you are discussing it with – you may find you need to provide them with some support in dealing with the nature of it.

If you have the time it may be worth sitting down with your tutor team and discussing key students and their profiles, whether that is in a 10-minute slot or an hour of inset time (if you are lucky!). It pays for your tutor team to know the year group and its most prominent or vulnerable students, as they can then also support each other when necessary.

Changing Tutors

It's very often the case that a tutor team put into place in Year 7, for example, won't be the same tutor team by the time those students leave the school. I can't think of a tutor team that has stayed the same through a 5-year cycle dating back to my own time at school. It is a fact that there is a chop-and-change of tutors in schools whether that is through staff leaving, being promoted, or retiring. It can be a real kicker to think you have established a strong tutor team and then learn that half of them are leaving or moving to positions in which they will no longer hold a tutor position. All that hard work for nothing.

Except if you have put the right strategies into place and held the highest standards, you should have created an environment in which a new tutor can slot into the tutor team and tutor group with little fuss. There will always be teething troubles and a settling-in period, but this is where you need to start your work again. Ensure that your new tutor is inducted well into the team. Provide them with all of the information you can about their tutor group, the tutor time schedule, where to find resources, who they can ask for support and any other information you feel is relevant. Let them settle in with their tutor group but watch from afar to ensure that everything is going okay and check in to see that there aren't any issues arising. If you are fortunate enough to know who is taking over a tutor group whilst their old tutor is still in the school, you should approach this carefully but capitalise on the fact there can be some form of transition/handover.

Everybody is different and will want to handle that situation differently, as a minimum I would suggest you set up a meeting with the ex-tutor and new tutor to share key information about the tutor group and point out resources/books etc. Having been in this situation as a tutor I was advised to visit the tutor group, introduce myself and stick around during their last week with their tutor. For me, this didn't feel right as I wanted to give their old tutor the chance to say goodbye and spend a last week with the tutor group also giving me the chance to have a fresh start in the same way as I would with a new class and not feel like I have to run with however the old tutor operated. This will differ on a case-by-case and person-by-person basis according to need – judge what you feel is best and what will result in the best reaction from the staff and tutees involved.

Moving Students to New Tutor Groups

Getting the balance of a tutor group right is a delicate and tricky activity – when students are placed into tutor groups/class groups upon joining the school it's a bit of a guessing game as to whether the groups you are building will work culturally with all of the individuals placed within it. For me when I think of classes I have found more difficult to teach during my career it is the case that they were all taught in tutor groups. There is a slight difference in the relationships of students and, often, those classes are together on a significant number of occasions during the week – so plenty of time to fallout and build bad habits!

As a Head of Year/Pastoral Leader you should always be looking at the balance of your groups and whether the right students are in the right groups with the right people. Do you have a tutor in your team who can build fantastic relationships with 'challenging boys' where a student might be better placed? A tutor who has significant experience of dealing with children with SEMH issues or SEND students? Tutor groups don't always need to remain static and where the need arises you should feel confident to make changes that are beneficial for individuals, classes or tutors. I find these decisions are often left until too late – that Year 7 form that every teacher knows is tough to teach because the balance of individuals within it isn't right should have some changes made to it as soon as that is realised. The Year 11 girl who has a fantastic relationship with one of your tutors whose attendance is dropping and may be more likely to attend if seeing a friendly face during the day. Also carefully consider where new entrants to the school are placed – who oversees this and are those decisions made around the best place for the student or as simply as the number of students in a tutor group?

If you do consider making this kind of change – always talk to the tutors it will affect first and think of the impact you will have on them. Part of that delicate balancing act is realising that what might be best for an individual could also upset the existing status quo and create more issues. I'd encourage you to think about where there are opportunities for you to balance your tutor groups. How do you go about analysing this? Is there an opportunity for you to discuss with tutors whether the make-up of their tutor group is working?

Circulate during Tutor Times/Non-Lesson Sessions

You are busy. All Pastoral Staff are. I can't stress enough though the importance of finding time to circulate to lessons and I feel it's just as important to do the same for tutor times or non-lesson sessions – perhaps more so than for standard lessons. If you don't know what is going on during these times then you can't judge whether they are useful, purposeful (and peaceful!) time slots for the children you are responsible for. There may also be situations in which your tutors, for example, could make use of your support and showing a united front on this will go a long way in helping your tutors to deal with incidents that arise in the future.

You clearly won't be able to visit every group, every day and there will be times when you can't visit any at all. In reality an aim to get into as many as you can, as often as you can, means you aren't stifling a tutor who wants to be the beacon for their group but also shows that you are present and supportive. It also allows you to spend a decent amount of time with a group if the opportunity arises, perhaps the chance to support a tutor in checking uniform or taking part in a news quiz or literacy activity. For some staff they may be uncomfortable with this and you should be careful not to overstay your welcome if you get the feeling you are making a tutor uncomfortable with your presence. You can always come back at a different date/time or have a discussion with the tutor to ensure they understand that you are not there to monitor them but to show their tutees that you are there to support.

Provide Rigour and Structure in Larger Events e.g. Assemblies, Fire Drills

Your tutors will appreciate rigour, structure and support around year group events that take place in public forums such as assemblies, fire drills or off-timetable days. Wherever possible, you want to create situations where tutors are the friendly face, encouraging students to do the right thing on these occasions – offering the advice to 'tuck your shirt in' or helping them tie a tie before walking into assembly. I always feel it is my job, or a member of the pastoral team, to then be the person who makes it clear that you listen to what your tutor has told you or you would find yourself falling into trouble.

Part of this means creating structures that allow tutors to perform that role and limit chances for students to get it wrong. If you insist that students are silent walking into assembly, for example, then routines should be introduced, and practicsed, where tutor groups line up outside the hall and will enter when silent – set the standard early and in your presence, and practise as often as needed, so that your tutors have to do a minimal amount of work. If the expectation is that students enter in silence but they then arrive after their tutor and the tutor then must settle them as they walk in and sit down you are setting them up to fail. If you have standards set for a fire drill, as another example, clearly articulate these to the year group and let tutors know exactly what you expect of them, alongside this. If you don't let tutors know that you want them to line students up, take the register in silence and then walk up and down the line promoting that silence, then you can't have complaints when they stand at the front keeping them in a straight line. Make it clear what your priorities are and then back tutors in enforcing them.

Acknowledge, Praise and Support

Finally, if you want to build a brilliant tutor team, remember that your tutors are all humans and they need praise when things are going well and support when they aren't.

Are there any opportunities you are currently missing to offer praise tutors?

Are there tutor group awards you could be giving out? Be careful around things like tutor group attendance where some tutors will simply never win due to the make-up of their forms but will likely be doing great work in another area.

Could you do something simple like writing a card for all of your tutors to thank them for their support during the year?

Can you speak to their line-manager or Head of Faculty to share how well they are doing with their tutor group or a tutee?

Questions to Ask of Yourself, Your Team, Your Staff, Your Students, or Your Wider Community

What experience do I have as an individual of leading others and how does this translate to pastoral care?

What qualifications or CPD could I undertake to further my leadership ability/capacity?

As a school, how much time is dedicated to sharing key pastoral information/concerns with staff at an individual/group level?

Do we empower our leaders at all levels to engage with pastoral data to better the areas they lead?

What would staff say about the support they receive from pastoral staff/leaders in the school? Do we survey this or take 360-degree feedback?

How has my experience as a tutor prepared me to lead a team of tutors? What have been the positive and negative experiences?

What makes a good tutor, in my opinion?

As a school, how do we developed our tutor staff and ensure they understand the expectations we have of them?

How do we establish tutor time routines and ensure that these are being followed?

How do we decide what activities to undertake during tutor time? How do we evaluate their successes?

How often do we survey student opinion on tutor time and the value of activities undertaken?

6   Behaviour Management

Behaviour management is, and always will be, a hot topic in education. The issue of how we manage the behaviour of students can be an incredibly polarising issue and, as with most polarising issues, there is always middle ground to be found.

Most schools tend to operate under variants of the same system with different levels of support, challenge and intervention usually driven by their contextual needs. In this chapter, I cover the wider strategic behavioural challenges the sector faces as well as bringing together practical advice, and my own experiences, to offer you strategies and tips on how to manage behaviour. This chapter is clearly not exhaustive and there are many strategies and ideas within it that may not land in your own specific context, as always, be a critical reader and determine whether what is presented here is useful to you, and, if you can adapt it to your own context.

Getting the Fundamentals Right for Everyone

You don't need to agree with the methods you use to manage behaviour in your school, provided they ensure that all students are kept safe and happy – that's what we are all striving for in the end. That being said I stand on the side of balance – children thrive upon consistency and predictability within their environment – in this they are no different to us as adults. They wish to understand the consequences for actions – some children learn this through our communication of it "Don't do this, or this will happen" and others have to experience it, or make the mistake, in order for the lesson to be learned. This is why there will always be a need for behaviour management systems of some kind which are clear to students, and staff, on the response to negative behaviours. Equally, we must balance this with the loving, caring approach to negative behaviours in which we show students that, despite making mistakes, the adults around them are prepared to help them navigate this.

As someone who has worked exclusively within challenging/deprived communities, I've been exposed to the lowest levels of disruption and some of the most extreme. The further you delve into the world of pastoral care the more varied this becomes – one moment you are dealing with a student who refuses to complete homework and the next it could be an assault; drugs; sexual abuse or any other range of issues you would wish our children weren't exposed to. On a daily basis, the plethora of inappropriate behaviours children are exposed to is on the rise. There are many things we could attribute this to; the scaling back of public services; the internet/social media or simply changes in attitude or parenting over time. Our job as pastoral staff is to be ready to respond to these issues and to do our utmost to prepare the children in our care for what is an increasingly less forgiving world.

Can One Size Fit All?

Ultimately, wherever you sit on the spectrum of opinion about how to manage behaviour, there should be an acceptance that the strategies that work successfully in one school/environment may not work within another. This further extends to trusts who take on schools in very different circumstances, where school X and school Y may need slightly different policies/procedures despite being a part of the same overall framework. I have yet to find a member of staff in a school whose desire is for children to be unruly, unsafe or unworkable; however, the difference of opinion on behaviour management often leads to this conclusion being drawn by those on opposite sides of the spectrum. Zero Tolerance vs Restorative Practise/Conversation are often where the lines are drawn in these battles and, honestly, there are very few schools which don't land somewhere in the middle.

The question arises of if there is an optimal approach to behaviour management and the only way I can answer that is to reflect on my own experiences. In the schools I have worked in and visited the best behaviour is exhibited in those where children unequivocally know where they stand. The phrase 'sweat the small stuff' crops up a lot with the ideal being that if you pick up on the smaller behaviour issues then the students will know that even the slightest misdemeanours are not tolerated and thus the larger ones definitely won't be!

In reality, it is another method for demonstrating consistency – different schools will 'sweat' different things, whether that is uniform, equipment, punctuality or even something more abstract such as manners. The important part is the consistency of the response – if I know, as a child, that the school will absolutely pick me up on wearing trainers and this has been demonstrated to me through the consistent actions of the school staff then I will hesitate to put them on in the morning in all but the most 'extreme' situations. We fall down as a school team when this consistency on behaviour management is not applied in all areas – this extends to all facets of the school day. It sounds like telling grandma how to suck eggs by saying that if we've told students about X rule then we need to ensure that X rule is followed – of course we do right? – but I can almost guarantee if you have an issue with students following that rule it's probably because somebody, somewhere is letting the system down and bringing inconsistency into your students' lives. Your job as a member of pastoral staff, or leadership, is to try and sniff that out.

It's worth, at this juncture, to issue a reminder to regularly review our policies, procedures and practises in this arena – a perfect example of this links to the issue discussed above around uniform. As a school/pastoral leader, uniform is important in setting boundaries/expectations for your school community but how often do we review it and check that it is appropriate and meets need? You only have to look in your local newspaper in September, without fail every year, to see a photo of a sad-faced child in their clearly inappropriate school uniform complaining about their school's draconian rules. The reality is that 95% of the time the parent involved has either made a mistake, or been convinced by their child, with regard to the uniform policy. There are other times, though where you will see a student isolated for a haircut too short or wearing shorts in 40-degree weather – it's those times that I question whether that school is meeting the needs of their community or merely enforcing the black and white rules of a uniform policy, which may be outdated. These occasions make it harder for staff to enforce policy, as it's hard to see the rationale behind it.

Ensuring Consistency and High Expectation with Visibility

Fundamentally, you need to be as visible as you possibly can – your visibility ensures that students see you addressing issues as they arise and also provides you with opportunities to check that behaviour is where you would wish it to be. Is it a great thing if you are on a break duty and a student drops litter on the floor? No of course it isn't, but it is an opportunity to re-enforce the point to that student and anyone else in the vicinity that this isn't something tolerated within the school – every behaviour misstep is an opportunity for correction and further development of the narrative, and this also goes for interactions with staff.

Depending on your role you may have the remit to remind staff of expectations, or you may need to escalate this to a senior member of staff, in an appropriate manner – nobody needs to be told off in the first instance as we all make mistakes. What you don't want to do is let misuse/management of your behaviour systems continue if you have spotted them. If the school policy is that students stand behind chairs at the end of a lesson and you see that a member of staff does not do this with their classes then this isn't something you should walk past – it needs challenging as it lets down the entire school team and, most importantly, the children as it adds an element of confusion about who is in the right.

There's no greater way to get the temperature for the school, or groups you are responsible for, than to pop into lessons and see how they are doing, rewarding any good behaviour/achievement and re-enforcing teacher expectations for those who aren't quite there yet. This might not be something you've done before, and it might take you a little while to feel comfortable knocking on somebody's door and asking if everything is alright. At the end of the day your job is to support staff and pupils and by being seen in/around lessons you will make it clear that you could arrive at any time which is a good motivator for some students - some of my favourite moments as Head of Year came when a teacher would welcome me into a room and speak glowingly about student's behaviour, their work or attitude.

Where appropriate, it's also wonderful to stick around and be a part of the lesson with students – often in pastoral care we deal with the negative and you should recognise any opportunity that arises to really enjoy being around the students in your care. Some of my favourite moments in pastoral leadership have arisen through just wandering into a lesson and sitting down next to a student for ten minutes and getting to be a part of the audience.

When it comes to those opportunities to enter classrooms, some teachers will see you as the answer to their prayers because you've walked into their worst class and you'll be immediately pointed to issues. If this is the case it likely isn't your job to deal with classroom behaviour issues – it's easy to be dragged into issues that would never have reached your door just because you walked in. Re-enforce the expectations of the school and the teacher but don't be tempted to try to 'fix' the issue by removing a pupil or doing something that wouldn't have occurred naturally within the school systems – this goes against what we've talked about with regard to consistency. Clearly there will be exceptions to this, and it may be appropriate for you to step-in but don't make that the norm as it will defeat the purpose of popping into lessons.

Other times you will be welcomed with open arms and pointed to students who are working well, classes that are fantastic, this is your opportunity to shower them with praise. It's a great opportunity to recognise the efforts of those students who are doing well and drag along those students who aren't quite there yet.

On occasions there will be times that a member of staff may feel uncomfortable with your presence in their classroom or area for any number of reasons(you may be interrupting their flow, they might be trying something new, they may be struggling with behaviour) – on these occasions I would tend to ask the following two questions, aloud, for the class to hear; "Good morning Sir/Miss/Mrs X, is everything going well this morning?" and "Is there anything I can do to help?" sometimes adding in a question about whether they were particularly pleased with any students. You'll quickly get the feel for the room – as a teacher, sometimes other people walk in at precisely the wrong time – if you think you've done that for any reason, don't feel the need to stick around, you can always come back a different day!

Visibility extends further into all aspects of the school. I made a point of going out on gate duty at every chance I got. It's a beautiful opportunity to say good morning/goodbye to your students and it's equally a time for you to catch any students you might have missed during the day and to speak to individuals about how their day was – particularly useful if you have students on report to you that are prone to 'forgetting' to come and see you. If your school doesn't have some sort of 'meet and greet' in the mornings, this could also be something to introduce. HOYs/SLT on the doors in the morning, greeting pupils, checking uniform, picking up issues from the previous day, giving out reports, etc. It takes 20–30 minutes out of your morning each day but is a real timesaver for those small 'chasing-up' jobs that we tend to push back throughout the day as we respond to more pressing issues which arise.

More suggestions to increase your visibility

- leave your office door open during the day when possible
- wander around the site at break/lunch times and interact with pupils
- attend/run extra-curricular events or evenings
- lead assemblies
- eat with the students at break/lunch once a week
- morning/After-School gate duties as students enter/leave

Reinforcing Your Message

The Head of Key Stage 4, when I started as Head of Year 10, was the first person I heard say, 'The standards you walk past are the standards you accept' and you need to live that if you work in pastoral care. If you walk past boys in the corridor with their ties off; if you ignore the girl in the lunch queue who pushed in, if you don't confiscate the basketball that's being bounced down the corridor then you are accepting these things and, consequentially, making it harder for the next member of staff who does choose to challenge this. Everything you do sends a message. It's not always easy. You might be dashing to a meeting, expecting a phone call, heading off to teach but as much as possible you need to live your standards and make sure that students know that they won't get anything past you – that you live the standards of the school. Take every opportunity as one to develop and demonstrate those standards, whether it's while you are grabbing a drink at break, welcoming students into assembly or popping into a lesson and don't miss out on those valuable learning experiences for the school community.

There is a downside to being visible – you end up dealing with more than if you hid from the world! Chances are if you are working, or aspire to be, in pastoral care you aren't somebody who wants to be sat down all day hidden away in the dark. You can't, however, be everything to everyone and there needs to be a balance here – pastoral teams in schools, we've established earlier, are now bigger than ever before. In order to be truly effective, you need to ensure that whatever your position within the team that there is an equitable approach to dealing with behaviour. It's easy to burn out in pastoral care, particularly if you find yourself firefighting poor behaviour or attempting to hold the line alone.

Case Study 6.1 Never Give Up

by Thomas Farnell
Safeguarding and Welfare officer at a grammar school in the West Midlands

James was a year 7 student. For the first few weeks in September, he was a model student. His teachers were really impressed with his work, he was engaged in the lessons; He seemed to have settled in really well.

One morning I got a call and was asked to go down to his form room. His tutor said that he had left his chair and had sat in the corner of the room, pulling chairs around him as a makeshift barricade. James's tutor had tried talking to him, but James would not respond, other than saying "paper". I introduced myself and asked him if he was okay. Again, he didn't talk. I sat down on the floor and started talking about myself, about school. I asked James if he would like to go for a walk so that we could talk. He nodded gently and got up. James started talking and opening up. We got to my office, and he gave me the note he had made. He wrote about having to go through family court and being stuck in the middle of his mom and dad. He talked about a lack of friends and thinking people didn't like him.

We got James's mom into school for a meeting. Mom said the family has "always been like that" so the note didn't make sense. Mom said they broke up when James was 3 or 4 and it had been a 'volatile relationship'.

This incident was the beginning of a downward spiral for James. Within a couple of weeks, incidents like this were happening two/three times a day. Each time, I would have to go to the class and sit on the floor next to him, sometimes for 10/15 minutes until he felt comfortable enough to leave. James would never talk when he was in this frame of mind. He would only respond with whimpers. He would curl up tightly in a ball and bury his face. As the term progressed this behaviour started evolving; he wasn't just sitting in a corner/under a desk now, if he was questioned or challenged at all he would run. Instead of spending 15 minutes on the floor, it was 15 minutes playing hide and seek. Teachers were struggling as his behaviour deteriorated and it was impacting the rest of the class.

This isn't a "happy ending" story. When James returned to school after the 2020 COVID lockdown, things appeared to be much better. After a few weeks, some issues started arising again, but not quite on the same scale, for now. We have tried getting support from external agencies, but it is proving difficult. The main thing is to never give up. No matter how frustrating it can be, never give up. I had days that were completely taken over, I spent more time sitting on the floor than a chair some days - but James was obviously going through something. The least I could do was make sure that he knew he was supported. I can only hope that one day all of the support we put into place will pay off with James trusting that we have his best interests at heart – my experience says that he probably will.

Real-Life Strategising

There are some areas of behaviour management within pastoral care that you will develop experience in as you spend more time in the role and that are only improved through longevity. There are other areas which you can immediately improve through the sharing of best practise and with the benefit of understanding other's learned tips/tricks. Here are some of mine for specific situations that might help you on your way

Confrontations

Nobody goes to work to deal with student fights/confrontations, but the reality is that they do happen, whether it's once in a blue moon or once a day. In a previous school my experiences were very much in the second of those two camps and I was given some advice, that I developed through my own experiences, which helped in managing those often-fraught situations. As a member of the pastoral team, you are clearly much more likely to be called to deal with these issues, usually as a result of a vague radio call or an out-of-breath student/staff member knocking on your door or grabbing you from the corridor.

...............................*Top Tip: Pause and Consider*...............................

When I first started out as an Assistant Head of Year and I was called to these situations, my temptation was always to get there as fast as possible and this is something I eventually realised didn't help me to de-escalate a situation. I always phrase this advice when talking to others as taking a considered approach to considering your approach. The time it takes you to respond to any situation can be used productively by considering how you will respond to/deal with the particular problem when you arrive. When I reflected on what happened when I raced to a situation to deal with it, I found that I'd arrive and then be firefighting from the get-go, as I hadn't considered what I was walking into. There is a reason that the police will hold a tactical briefing before entering into a situation they know is likely to be fraught – it avoids the headless chicken response.

I really clearly remember being told about a fight at the local shops and sprinting there, across the field, through the estate to the wrong place, then sprinting again to the right place and realising on arrival that my out-of-breath Ultimate Warrior impression *(one for the wrestling fans)* meant I didn't have much chance of calmly resolving the situation. If you give yourself time to think as you are en-route you can consider what you are going to say/do when you arrive; How will you break up the students? Can you stop into an office on the way there to get support? How will you disperse a crowd that's gathered? What will you do if you can't resolve it alone? What information have you been given that could help you?

As a sidenote, if ever you do find yourself trying to break up a fight alone (not something I would encourage but sometimes they appear on top of us!) it's often the case that one participant wants to be there much less than the other. A tool/phrase I'd often use would be to figure out who was the one who wanted to be there least, direct my attention to the aggressor and instruct them very clearly and authoritatively to walk away (anywhere, it doesn't particularly matter for now, as long as they are away from the victim, as they can be picked up later) after getting into a position where the other student is safer, usually behind me. Again, never something I'd encourage, but sometimes we find ourselves in these positions due to the nature of the role and it's good to at least have some idea of what we can do.

Taking Statements

Pastoral roles are odd. You can go from delivering an assembly, teaching a maths lesson, or meeting a parent into investigating the latest incident in the long-running case of 'The Toilet Terroriser'. I'm fairly sure if I ever wanted to join the police, I'd have plenty of investigative experience to talk about! While this is easy to joke about there is a fundamental need for the statementing of incidents and for there to be clear records, particularly of higher profile issues, that arise within schools. There is always the potential that records of a behaviour incident could be useful, or needed, in events in the future and so accurately and expertly recording these is of great importance.

.... *Top Tip: The Far-Reaching Value of Accurate Records*............

This stretches into many different fields and a couple of examples demonstrate this perfectly. As a school governor, I have, as part of a panel, overturned a permanent exclusion in which the statements taken did not accurately reflect the information needed to make a decision on this scale. In another example, a student was involved in a serious accident which resulted in an unfortunate, permanent injury – investigation at the time showed that the student was being silly and statements all reflected this. Around five years later, legal action was taken against the school/local authority as it was claimed that the injury occurred as a result of bullying – the statements had all been recorded and kept and clearly refuted this – including the student's own statement. Equally, you may be asked to provide your statements to the police when an incident is reported to them and they have a need to investigate so it's best to ensure you get your processes right the first time around.

Whenever you have to undertake the process of taking statements, or recording an incident in the case of younger students, it's always a balancing act – we all go into education-based roles because we want the best for children and as a result we are often predisposed to believe them and believe that they wouldn't willfully break rules. Children naturally don't want to get into trouble and sometimes these are less statement and more interrogations and it's good to have some tools in the locker that make this process less painful for you. Nothing is worse than spending a good chunk of your day taking statements and then somebody contradicts what's been said and you have to go all the way back to the beginning.

Tool 1: Question Their Loyalty

If you've never heard the phrase "I ain't snitching on my mates" or "I ain't saying nuffin", count yourself lucky. The best way I've found to counter this is to remind students that there are x number of other students all sat, or about to be sat, giving statements to members of staff. Ask them if they can be sure that they are all saying the same thing, ask them if they are sure that their 'mates' aren't going to try to get out of trouble by saying somebody else is responsible.

Tool 2: Remind Them That This Is Their One Opportunity to Set the Record Straight

I always lead with the mantra with students that I'd be much happier to find out that they had made a silly mistake the first time I asked, rather than the second, third or fourth, and that if I spent more time on something because I was lied to then sanctions would always factor this in. When taking statements, I always make sure to let students know that the statement they give is the statement that I will work with and that any time you change what you say will make you much less likely to be believed in the future. This is also useful for your own investigative purposes if you have to return to a student as you can read back to them multiple versions of statements that they have provided/written in their own words.

Tool 3: Have a Lengthy Statement in Your Drawer from a Previous Incident

"I didn't see anything" signed by John Smith on the first line of a piece of paper is always frustrating after giving a student the opportunity to give their version of events. On some occasions when students did this I would ask them if they were happy with the length of their statement and then take a lengthy statement out of my drawer from a previous incident (usually two sides), show it from a distance and then inform the student that other statements that I'd taken were significantly longer and much more detailed. It's all well and good writing one line if you think that's what everyone is doing, when presented with the idea that others might be writing a lot more it sometimes prompted a more honest account.

Tool 4: Write Statements Yourself

This one is particularly for situations where you know it may escalate to an internal/external exclusion, will be used in parental meetings etc. but I think is good practise regardless, if you have the time. As time-consuming as it is, I'd always encourage you to take and write statements yourself from students as it's usually the case that when they are tasked with writing them themselves they conveniently leave out details we already know about and are less likely to tell the truth. You want to be in a position where you can prompt for answers but not ask leading questions "Was somebody in the toilets? If I check the CCTV will I see somebody walk in?" rather than "Jeremy was in the toilets, wasn't he". More than anything this will help to ensure that statements are clear, contain the level of detail needed and are in a logical order for anybody else who may read them. By writing them yourself you also have the opportunity to re-question once certain comments have been committed to paper to see if a student has any further information to add.

Tool 5: I Already Know Everything!

I've had great success in resolving incidents by letting students I already know what happened, who was involved, etc. (when I actually know nothing) and that all I'm testing now is whether the student I am speaking to is going to be honest or not. I can make it clear that if they are honest, and the story they tell me matches the 'truth' I already have, that their sanction may be lessened or that the burden isn't on them as the only person who is discussing it. This is always a bit of a gamble and best suited for a situation where you know the students quite well but that they may reticent to provide you with information if they think it is going to get somebody else in trouble – this takes the pressure off of them in divulging the information.

Responding to Classroom Incidents/On-Call or Referral Systems

Whatever your context you will likely have some sort of on-call, referral or removal system in which a class teacher can request the support of another member of staff (usually a teaching/pastoral middle leader or SLT). As strange as it might sound, I always enjoy taking on this role – if you take it as an opportunity to spend an hour walking around the building, popping into lessons and being given the opportunity to interact, and build relationships, with some of the most difficult students in your school then it can be incredibly rewarding. The days where you get 10–15 calls in an hour though I will say aren't as rewarding!

.... *Top Tip: Benefitting from Calm De-escalatio*....................

When I left my previous school, a member of staff chose that moment to tell me that they thought I was too nice to students when I was called to on-call incidents. I apparently didn't shout enough – something that I have seen as an expectation before. Some staff expect that when you arrive, you are there to bring a child to the verge of tears to make them understand the error of their ways. I've always seen my role in these situations as the opposite – a child has gotten themselves into a situation that they either regret or will likely regret if given space away from it and it's my job to facilitate de-escalation. People will often criticise you for taking a child away for a 'nice chat' after they've misbehaved without understanding that there are a multitude of factors at work here – we are trying to repair a relationship with the child for them; we are trying to calm down a child to the point they can reflect and discuss the incident with clarity rather than anger or even that we can see something else is at play and we need to figure out what.

The scenario I've listed below is an example of a go-to approach/structured response that I used to address a specific classroom-based problem, after which I was told that I should have raised my voice and insisted the rules were followed.

Scenario: The Student Who Won't Leave the Room

At a previous school there was a spate of students refusing to leave the room when a member of staff was called to remove them. It's all well and good me saying my role is de-escalation but if the student won't even leave the room to discuss their behaviour – how can I help them/the member of staff? This was one of the biggest frustrations I faced early on as an Assistant Head of Year. After a few failed attempts (and questioning if I had the mettle to work in pastoral care) when faced with this issue I stuck to a particular script that worked on one occasion and after noticing it worked a majority of the time after that. If I'd asked a student to leave and they refused (whether politely or not as politely I'd like) I'd inform them that I'd give them a minute to consider whether that was a sensible decision for them to make and then tell the class teacher I was popping to deal with a call next door or similar. I'd return in exactly one minute and if the student still refused, I'd move into the room and crouch down next to them and very quietly say something similar to the following:

> I know there is a reason you don't want to leave the room, but I can't help you in here, I need to be able to talk to you outside of this environment. Nobody in this room knows what I'm telling you at this point, for all they know I'm telling you that if you don't leave the room, you will be permanently excluded, let them think whatever they want. Let's get out of here and go for a walk so that I can help you.

I can't remember a student refusing to leave the room with me after I started to implement that strategy. Sometimes it's because they have their excuse to not lose face in front of their peers, sometimes it's because you've moved into their space and aren't just a figure at the door telling them to get out or they realise you aren't going away. Usually, it's because they recognise that you are there to help them navigate their way out of the situation they have worked themselves into – most of the time when a situation has reached a boiling point with a student they really want to find a way to walk that back.

The following case study is a, somewhat humorous, reflection on the random and surprising incidents which can befall you when dealing with behaviour in schools and the need to always reflect on your approach to a situation.

Case Study 6.2 Having Your Wits about You

In an ICT lesson that I was supporting as a Teaching Assistant, a teacher had sent a Year 8 boy out of the room for continually causing distractions with a rubber lizard. He rang reception for the on-call duty member to come down and remove the student. I, being the diligent and caring member of staff that I am and desperate to do more pastoral work, decided to go out and check on the student. I was greeted by an orange which, thrown full force, just missed me and hit the wall. Slightly perplexed by what had just happened I took a moment to process, as the member of staff on duty turned the corridor. He had a conversation with the student firstly about why he had thrown an orange at me, before asking why he was being removed. He apologised, he thought it was the teacher who was coming out of the door, which, in his head, clearly made it okay. The duty staff member made very clear why this wasn't something the school tolerated and stressed just how serious his actions were and told him to go and pick up the orange while asking me to fetch the teacher – here was error number one. Relieved that I wasn't the target of the fruit-based, attempted assassination I returned to the classroom to get the member of staff so that he could inform duty of why the student needed to be removed. Here was error number two on the part of the duty staff – he hadn't confiscated the orange. Having practiced once, the student had honed his craft and his aim was much improved. On exiting the room, the unfortunate teacher was also greeted by the same orange – this time a perfect, devastating headshot. I don't quite know what happened in that corridor after I left it, but the teacher was never the same again. He returned to the classroom; the student had been removed but the scars of that day remained – largely due to the fact everyone in the faculty office took great pleasure in leaving orange related items on his desk. The lesson to be learned here? If you are called to a lesson on duty always confiscate any fruit you see. No, wait, don't assume that students will do as you've told them? Appraise yourself of all of the facts before you deal with a situation? If a student has a rubber lizard, leave them well alone? I guess it's just a cautionary tale about having your wits about you at all times in pastoral care and being ready for the unexpected!

Take a Walk

I've spent a lot of my time in pastoral care working in particular with boys to try and develop positive behaviours, having spent two and a half years at a boys' school, and one of the things that I found useful in a lot of situations is going for a walk. Whether it's to calm them down or get them talking, the different environment and the fact you are moving helps to change the situation positively. It's something that is spoken about quite frequently now, putting boys into low-pressure situations where it's easier to talk because you aren't sat directly across from each other in which can sometimes be awkward or uncomfortable.

......................*Top Tip: Never Underestimate Fresh Air*......................

It's much easier to open up in a seemingly lower pressure environment where you aren't sat opposite each other and there are other things in the environment to focus their attention on – other times they will start talking just because they want to get in out of the cold if you take a walk in the fresh air! I tend to like to go outside if I offer a student the chance to take a walk wherever possible – a lap around the building, sitting on a bench on the way, etc. We all feel a little bit better for getting some fresh air and it's something I'd suggest you try if you find yourself in a situation where you are trying to get a student talking or calm.

Again – to be judged according to your context – I wouldn't take a student outside of the building if I felt they might be a danger or at risk of running off site. My anecdotal experience suggests boys and girls respond differently here and that while both genders appreciate a walk as an opportunity to calm down – girls seem to be more appreciative of conversations behind closed doors or in a familiar space. Obviously, this isn't true of all cases and may not be anything other than my own anecdotal experience but I'd encourage you to test out the theory and see how students react in your own environment.

Breathing

The final strategy I want to talk about is perhaps the simplest but it's one that changed the way I deal with upset/angry students completely. I can't for the life of me remember when or why I started but my instinct says I read something that made me say "Oh... well that makes a ridiculous amount of sense" and adopted it ever since.

Think back to any time you've dealt with a student who was worked up, agitated, angry or upset. They may be tearful, pacing around or shouting. One thing that is usually common is that their breathing is erratic and contributing to their agitated state. Equally, students who are currently focusing negative energy or aggression towards an outburst need to have their focus directed elsewhere and switching it onto their breathing is an excellent distraction.

................................*Top Tip: And Breathe*................................

It's no exaggeration at this point in my career to say that I have been in countless situations where changing a student's focus to their breathing before attempting to address a situation has completely altered the outcome. It seems small and potentially insignificant, but I can't credit it enough. As adults, we tend to be better at this – how often have you been in a challenging/difficult situation and told somebody you need to go outside for a breather. I've seen situations where students are upset, breathing heavily and pacing around while somebody tries to talk to them or offer advice – it's so often futile because the child isn't in a position to be open to this.

If you find yourself in a situation with a student who you feel could benefit and where you can see that their breathing is heavy or irregular, tell them to focus on you, whether that's looking at you or closing their eyes and listening to your voice. Tell them you are going to ask them to take a big breath in through their nose, they need to hold it and then release when you say after a couple of seconds "Big breath in through your nose, hold it, out through your mouth" and do this 5-10 times. Change your wording then to "big breath in…and out" and then eventually to just "in..and out" before you ask them to keep going without you saying anything. In younger children, and sometimes with older children, it's a good idea to model it and breathe with them at the start before you work your way through into words and then letting them control their own breathing. There are a number of other breathing strategies you can find online which focus on tracing your fingers, counting objects in the room, etc. which you can utilise also depending upon the needs/age of the child. Once you can see that their breathing has changed, you should still give them a minute or so to adapt back into their usual breathing rhythm – don't assume just because they aren't breathing like they've just run a marathon that they are back to normal. Eventually, you should see them visibly begin to calm through the process and then you can begin to start to try and talk to them.

Rewards/Praise

It is always the case that when we discuss behaviour, we disproportionately discuss the negatives versus the positives – that is evident so far in this chapter of my book with the amount of words dedicated to general/specific behaviour management practices. It is important not to forget the role that rewards/praise play in the effective management of behaviour in schools.

It is, obviously, our goal in schools to reduce as much poor behaviour as possible to ensure that our learning environments are calm, safe places to be. Rewards and praise play a vital role in developing this culture and you should give clear though to your rewards strategy as a school. This doesn't necessarily need to all be based around intrinsic reward or items which you have to purchase/pay for to present to students but it should carefully consider your community/context and what holds value to them. Rewards systems which work in one context, as with all school strategies, may not work in yours. I once saw a fantastic alternative provision for students with Social, Emotional and Mental Health needs, which had a trophy cabinet on display in the centre of the school with a range of prizes inside, chosen by their community, and which could be earned by achieving a certain number of star points. This worked phenomenally well for them but would not scale up to a 1500-pupil secondary school.

Many of the best rewards systems focus primarily on recognition and on students feeling 'seen' and acknowledged for the good behaviour or contribution to the school. The vast majority of students will appreciate a certificate, praise points for good work, a phone call or postcard home or any other typical/traditional low-cost school reward. What is most important is that this system is consistent and fair.

Students rebel against reward systems which are wishy-washy or that reward students with typically poor behaviour. Think carefully about any rewards system you introduce and the capacity you have to ensure it runs as you envisioned. I am guilty of this myself having, in a previous school, recognised that our rewards policy was lacking and so introduced a huge system which involved multi-faceted rewards being implemented across the school. The reality was that neither I, nor the teaching staff required to push it, had the capacity at that point to really make it work and so it becomes more detrimental than positive. We scaled back and ensured that we gave out a form of the week and pupil of the week(with runners up) certificate each week, alongside subject certificates each half term – this was manageable, and appreciated, and worked as a platform to build on further.

Exclusions/suspensions

Finally, I wouldn't be doing a chapter on behaviour management justice if I didn't briefly talk about exclusions/suspensions. The polarisation of the issue often makes discourse around exclusion difficult, and it is one of the most emotive topics to discuss. Exclusion is a tool within a school's toolkit for the most serious sanction – it should not be used for anything other than this. There are, of course, times in schools when one child must be excluded to keep the majority safe or to uphold policies designed to do so. There should always be a recognition that exclusion is the last resort and that we should attempt every other strategy within our toolkit before actioning this serious sanction. To not exclude in the most serious of circumstances is to tell other students within your school that their safety is unimportant.

That being said exclusion is a blunt and often ineffective tool in changing the behaviours of the student being excluded – suspensions very often do little to effect chance and permanent exclusions we can often see coming sometimes years before they occur. This is the issue with the exclusion system. It needs to be the case that exclusion, as a last resort, remains an option for schools. We also need to do more to capitalise upon the experience of outstanding pupil referral units and alternative provisions at an earlier stage – as an experienced pastoral leader it's often easy to spot where a child would benefit from a provision that is not mainstream school and yet we often have to go through the motions of ensuring that a child has had every sanction possible, every method of support possible and every level of meeting in the framework of the local authority/trust. This often prolongs the time students with genuine difficulties are expected to exist within an environment that is not right for them. I would like to see a world where more funding is made available for specialist support at a much earlier stage for students and I believe this would ultimately reduce the need for exclusion to a point when it can be used for its only real purpose – as the most serious sanction a school can issue.

This chapter could run for the remainder of this book – it could be the entirety of this book. There are people much smarter/well-researched than I who have already done this. My goal with this chapter is to reflect the diversity of behaviour management strategies and expectations which come with a role in pastoral care. Equally, you will have seen that the ability to effectively manage behaviour does not come quickly – it is developed through time, experience, and reflection. There is no one-size-fits-all behaviour policy and no one way to deal with behaviour issues – it's up to you to work within the boundaries of your school's policy and to ensure that you do the best that you can for the children in your care.

Case Study 6.3 High Expectations

by Amy Forrester
Director of Behaviour in a Secondary School

High expectations matter. Very few teachers would disagree with the notion that high expectations of students are vital in schools. However, the reality of high expectations needs tenacity and perseverance. Why? Because they need to be upheld at every given opportunity. After all, if you let a child off, you let them down.

It can sometimes feel that letting a child off with a misdemeanour is a kindness; they've had a bad day, a bad week, or something significant has happened in their life. It can feel like you want to let them off because you care about the difficult they're facing. But this is fundamentally misguided.

> When you lower your expectations of a child, you're saying you don't believe in them; you don't think they can meet them. And that isn't kind or fair, despite how we might sometimes feel.
>
> In practice, this means unwavering use of school behaviour systems, of following sanctions that are set out by the school. That too can feel like an unkindness. But what would be unkinder is letting students grow up believing that it's acceptable to lower your standards of yourself because of what's happening in your life, to believe that life will cut you a break. That isn't the world they will grow up into as adults, and the greatest kindness we can do is to support them, with love and care, to meet those expectations, and to navigate their lives when they do let themselves down. Which they will because they're teenagers. Very few of us could claim we've never behaved in a way that doesn't meet our usual standard - we deal with the consequence of that. Children need to be taught this, too.
>
> So, next time a child doesn't meet your expectations, and that niggling doubt of "it would be easier to ignore that" creeps in, think twice. Is it the greatest kindness you can do? Will you be letting them down? And, because the answer will be yes, and you're dealing with children, make sure that your words and actions come from the heart, with care and love, and ensure that you are absolutely clear with a child that you're holding them to high expectations because you care. They might not see that right now, but years of working in pastoral care teaches me, without question, that they will in the long run. They'll thank you for it as they walk out of the door on their last day when they shake your hand and thank you for never giving up on them. They know they were worth your time and energy; what greater gift could you give to a child?

Questions to Ask of Yourself, Your Team, Your Staff, Your Students and Your Wider Community

What would our school look like if behaviour were at its best all the time? What is the ultimate goal for behaviour in this school in the long term?

Does our behaviour policy meet the needs of our community and our local context?

Does what's written in our behaviour policy translate into practise in the reality of the school day?

Is our behaviour policy accessible to all member of our community? Are key messages communicated in different languages/simply enough?

Is our behaviour policy created in isolation or do we consult key stakeholders in its creation?

How do we review our behaviour policy and whether it is appropriate/meets our needs?

How involved are our governing body in the shaping of this policy?

How often do we review the appropriateness of our uniform policy and the impact it has on our community?

Are the consequences of poor behaviour understood by all of the school community?

Are we clear on what poor behaviour looks like and how staff should address it?

Do we communicate this through different mediums, or do we expect the community to 'just know it'?

How do we/would we deal with concerns/suggestions raised around the use/implementation of the behaviour policy?

How do we communicate changes to the behaviour policy to our community and how do ensure those changes have been heard?

What are the behaviours we wish to see less of in our school environment? What are the positive behaviours we would like to see more of?

How do we reward positive behaviour and how do we check that these rewards are valued by the children receiving them?

How do we quality assure the use of rewards by staff and ensure that there is parity in the system?

Whose responsibility is it to manage behaviour in the school? The classroom? During unstructured time? Outside of school?

Are our procedures for investigating issues/incidents transparent and would they stand up to scrutiny?

How do we ensure that students are treated equally when sanctions are issued/how do we ensure that individuals/groups of students do not receive disproportionate sanctions due to things outside of their control?

Are our policies/practises around behaviour management inclusive for children with SEND? And EAL students?

Which student groups are most affected by exclusion/suspension in our school – what are we doing to try and address this?

How are sanctions/rewards communicated to students/parents?

Do we inform staff of how behaviour issues they have reported/flagged have been resolved?

7 Attendance/Punctuality

Attendance and Punctuality are two sides of the same coin – we often find that those students who have issues with their attendance similarly have issues with punctuality. Both of these areas, like much of the work we do, are so dependent on clear, concise systems that are easy for staff, students and parents to understand.

The benefit of simple systems is that they are equally as simple to action. Attendance and Punctuality systems fall down where they are too complex or are not effectively communicated.

Within this chapter, you'll find practical tips for supporting with increasing your school/trust attendance, gleaned from my time as a member of the pastoral team and as a Director of Attendance and Punctuality. In 2024, we have seen a significant push from the government in the UK on increasing attendance as we bounce back from COVID and, rightly, ensuring that students are in schools/classrooms to receive support. Without consistent attendance at school we are falling at the first hurdle.

The Value of a Whole School policy

The first, and most important element, of attendance and punctuality management is to ensure that you have a whole school policy that clearly outlines the expectations around attendance for students within the school.

Most schools will adapt their policy from one shared by a local authority, trust or best practise source. If you are in a position to then it's always a good idea to develop this policy in consultation with key stakeholders to ensure that it meets the needs of your context. There is no point in having a policy that is not practicable in reality and the staff who deal with attendance issues in your school should be able to have confidence that the policy matches the practise. If this is the case it is important still that you are clear on the implications of the policy and that all key staff involved in translating the policy into actions are similarly cognisant of its application.

Consistency arises again here and is a fundamental element of successful attendance strategies within school, as you will need to ensure that strategies outlined within your policy are consistently applied in the vast majority of situations within your school. There will clearly be, as there are with all elements of pastoral care, areas where you should adapt/tweak your attendance policy given contextual information but, for the vast majority of scenarios, it should be the case that you stick to it to the letter to ensure equity for all.

Your policy should clearly state the expectations for attendance within the school/trust and also the actions that will be taken at each stage as attendance drops and it's a good idea to produce a short 'explainer' document that can be shared during attendance meetings, displayed prominently in the school, etc. to ensure that the message on attendance is frequently communicated. Once you have a clear and suitable policy in place then you need to ensure that this is enacted throughout the school and reviewed regularly.

Mitigating Factors and Measuring Attendance

Improving attendance is an area that many schools struggle with – there is often a core contingent of students whose attendance issues just cannot be shifted. When I talk throughout this chapter about students with attendance issues, I will most often be referring to those students who do not attend their school through choice rather than students with genuine medical reasons for non-attendance. This distinction is important to make at this point; however, it does not mean that we should ignore those students whose attendance at school is prohibited by their medical needs – in reality, we need to ensure that our attendance policies and procedures are inclusive for them also. There are a number of factors, some given below, which may impact student attendance and you should always try to be aware of any of these possibilities in your diagnosis of an issue:

- Medical/health needs
- Bullying
- Confidence/self-esteem
- Anxiety
- Religious observance
- Exclusion/suspension

- Socio-economic factors/deprivation/familial education levels
- Academic issues
- SEND/EAL

One of the elements of your policy should be a graduated response to attendance issues – what happens when a student's attendance drops to 98%, 96%, 94%, etc. If you leave these things up to chance or the whims of the person dealing with this on a given day you are setting yourself up to fail and ensuring that your attendance systems will not work. An example of the approach you could take is given here:

Attendance	What does this mean?	Action
100%	Your child has excellent attendance	• Monitored by Tutor/Head of Year • Half-termly postcard/certificate for outstanding attendance and punctuality are posted home
96–99%	Your child has good attendance but could become a concern	• Monitored by Tutor/Head of Year/Attendance Officer

If your child's attendance drops below 96% (our whole school target), you will receive a letter notifying you that we will be monitoring your child's attendance. Our first concern is ensuring your child gets a quality education and this can only be done through regular school attendance.

90–95%	• Your child's attendance is a concern • This is the equivalent of between ½ a day to 1 day absent per fortnight	• If your child's attendance falls below 95% they will be monitored as a concern during weekly attendance meetings. • Letters escalating through our attendance policy will be sent home (reflective of your child's attendance) to improve attendance. • Strategies may be put into place in school to improve your child's attendance. • Absence for medical reasons will require medical evidence (doctors note, prescription proof, etc.) before authorisation.

(Continued)

Attendance/Punctuality

Attendance	What does this mean?	Action
	If your child's attendance fails to improve, they will be placed on an attendance support plan and you may be invited into school. Your case may be passed on to our Educational Welfare Officer, who will take further action to address your child's attendance, which could, ultimately, result in prosecution for non-school attendance/unsatisfactory school attendance.	
Below 90%	• Your child's attendance is a serious concern • Your child is classed as a 'Persistent Absentee' • This is the equivalent of more than ½ a day absent per week	• Meeting with the EWO/Head of Year • Attendance Support Plan set up in school • Fixed Penalty Notice (where appropriate) • Court Action (where appropriate)

The above is by no means the answer for every context but that isn't the point – we want to be in a situation where every stakeholder in the school community is clear of the action taken when attendance drops to certain levels, alongside the praise that is offered for good attendance. There will be many different viewpoints about where to draw the line on attendance percentages and when intervention/action/support should be offered – the important thing is to ensure that all staff, students and parents understand your policy.

Using 'Over' Communication as a Tool

If you are clear on the actions taken by the school for poor/deteriorating attendance, then you can begin to do the most important thing here – over-communicate. Having led attendance and increased communication with parents, you would be surprised how little knowledge there is amongst the community of the impact of poor attendance and how a day off here and there can stack up in the long run. Initially, when I did this there was lots of opposition to increased communication – parents resented the fact that their child's attendance was being put into context, having previously only been informed of the percentage. Suddenly adding in that 95% meant X hours of lost learning, providing the average attendance for their child against their year group or a comparison to a previous term rather than a yearly average was an affront.

I was regularly challenged, complained to, and chastised for sending information parents deemed unnecessary – on one occasion a child came into school with the letter I'd sent home and handed it back to me with a message from her dad to "not send anymore letters, they'd go straight into the recycling as it's all bullshit anyway" – environmentally conscious at least!

All of the above however, paled in comparison to the parents grateful for the communication and for whom the focus on attendance was greatly appreciated. My preferred model is to send an introductory letter at the start of the year, which outlines the school's attendance policy and informs parents of how to report absence, etc. This should then be followed up with a termly attendance update for each individual child, offering some of the contextual information discussed above. Throughout the year, attendance should also be discussed in newsletters, at parents' evenings and in more generic letters home.

Keeping Staff Informed

You also need to capitalise on the ability of your staff to support the drive for great whole school attendance by regularly sharing attendance/punctuality updates and making them aware of key elements of the attendance policy. Staff should be aware of the thresholds given in the policy for attendance intervention so that they, too, can have conversations with students and parents where relevant. They should understand how persistent absence is calculated and should be able to spot the signs of this and work together with you to remind students that X days off means a drop into classification as a persistent absentee. If we know that student X will become a persistent absentee for this term with one more day off, then we need to regularly communicate this with him and his parents/carers and praise his attendance whenever we can. If he then takes that day off, then we need to ensure we switch more intensive resources to students who we are capable of stopping from dropping into PA, whilst still trying to improve student X's attendance.

Assigning Key Staff and Expectations

Next on the list is ensuring that your systems for management of attendance work for your context – who are the staff you ask to manage attendance and do they see this a key part of their role or simply an added distraction?

Lots of schools now have separate attendance staff just for this purpose, for whom their sole focus is on receiving absence calls/emails; following up on absence after X number of days; creating/generating data and reports to be used by them and other key staff and attending meetings with parents/external agencies regarding student attendance. Ultimately, the accuracy of your absence systems is a safeguarding priority – you need to ensure, clearly, that you know where students are and why they are not in school. The longer you leave these conversations or the later you chase the missing mark from period 3, the more confusion you add into the process and the more difficult it is to establish whether a student was/is/is expected to be in school – and this is where you hit rocky ground in terms of safeguarding.

Prioritise accuracy of your registers in school and ensure that staff are clear that this is one of the most important jobs in their day – registers should be completed audibly with students responding to staff clearly to ensure that no mistakes are made. Absence texts that go out to parents who know they sent their child to school, due to an issue on a register, can cause real issues in schools, never mind the heart-stopping moment for a parent who now thinks their child's whereabouts are unknown!

Is It Working?

The package you offer to improve attendance will have a wide span and there are a number of strategies which you can undertake to try and achieve this. The big question is what will work for your context and you need to be agile in your response to this – if something isn't working you need to evaluate whether you think it's worth persisting with or whether what you've seen so far suggests it is unlikely to in the future. Which of the elements of the list below are included within your school's attendance 'provision'?

- Transition visits, which factor in children's attendance to their current stage of education and allow you to start to work with, and plan for, those students with a history of poor attendance before they reach your school
- Pre-visits to your school/environment for students with attendance issues

- Allocating a key member of staff to students with issues around anxiety, medical conditions, etc. which have made attendance difficult for them
- Outlining the school's attendance management procedures in a clear and easy-to-read format for students and parents
- Publicising the school's attendance and attendance targets prominently and regularly
- Sharing individual student attendance with parents on a regular basis, with comparative averages at a national and local level
- Breakfast clubs to encourage attendance at school and particularly improve punctuality
- Late gates/duty staff so that students who are late are challenged on the reasons for this
- Sanctions for poor punctuality
- Attendance/punctuality reports
- Attendance/punctuality initiatives and interventions
- Work with external agencies focusing on attendance such as Educational Welfare Officers
- Outreach work with students struggling to attend school
- Letters/communications that keep parents informed of the school's attendance policy
- Sharing attendance/punctuality data/information with class teachers/tutors responsible for student's pastoral care
- Rewarding students for excellent attendance/punctuality
- Re-integration from absence meetings/timetables that allow students to settle in gently
- Key staff responsible for attendance/punctuality

The likelihood is that you will do most of the above in some format or another – the question is whether you are confident that the time spent on these things is worth it or whether there are areas, proven by data, that have had a demonstrable impact on improving attendance/punctuality within your context. If so, then these are clearly the areas where you should be spending more time or instructing your staff to focus on further.

No Need for Absolute Perfection

You will note that at no point have I mentioned 100% attendance rewards/certificates. There has been a small shift in recent years to recognise that 100% attendance rewards do not promote a positive physical/mental well-being agenda. As an adult, it is clear to me that if I do not feel well enough to go to work, or that my attendance at work could be detrimental to the health of others, that I should not go in and should spend the time recuperating to return to my best. Why should this be any different for our children?

In many scenarios, children are not the ones responsible for their own attendance and many of the interventions and activities written about above focus primarily on educating parents on the impact of poor attendance. On the other side of this are students with longer-term medical/mental health issues for whom 100% attendance is not remotely achievable. As pastoral/school leaders I would suggest that you have three options – don't issue rewards for 100% attendance at all (and particularly do not base rewards events/trips, etc. on attendance); factor in students with known medical conditions in these decisions and ensure that no student is penalised for genuine medical conditions or issue your attendance certificates/rewards on a much smaller window, i.e. 100% attendance for the week = entry into a draw.

There are so many things that we can reward our students for and, whilst it is difficult in the current climate of attendance management, we must ensure that our practise around this is not discriminatory.

When it comes to punctuality, the approach should broadly be the same and again is built upon a level of consistency. Students need to know the consequences of being late not only from a sanctions perspective but also the consequences in terms of lost time. Communicating this with parents is often more effective as they do not realise that those 5 minutes of lateness in the morning can stack up to either a lot of lost learning time, disruption to the classroom or in their child missing key messages given out at the start of the day. You should be monitoring punctuality data regularly and again picking up patterns which show which students are regularly late – there is equally a split conversation to be had here about lateness to school and lateness to lessons, although this is primarily a distinction made at secondary school.

Ultimately, attendance in schools is a difficult and often stubborn issue to deal with. What you must be clear on is your role as an individual in any attendance management systems to ensure that children are kept safe and accounted for whether in, or out of, school. Post-COVID pandemic there is, rightly, an increased focus on the importance of good attendance to school and ensuring that you meet both statutory/legal obligations, as well as undertaking good practise, is more important than ever.

> ### Case Study 7.1 Consider the Child
>
> by John S
> Parent of Two Primary Age Children
>
> As a parent of two primary school age children, attendance at school is something that we take very seriously. Their school regularly communicates the importance of good attendance and the impact any time off from school can have on the learning of children. You would think then that as parents we would be celebrating the success of our children in receiving excellent attendance certificates – for those students with 95% or above attendance – except only one of my children did. The other has had some regularly bouts of sickness – nothing serious, thankfully, but enough to keep him off school and, as parents, we felt we were doing the responsible thing.
>
> We always back the school with praise and our children love to receive rewards from the school – whether that's a certificate, stickers, or any other form of reward that they regularly receive. The fridge is full of their accolades, and they love adding to it. That's why it was hard for us when our eldest received his attendance certificate and our youngest didn't – he couldn't understand why his brother was being rewarded for not being sick – something he had no control over. We could talk to him about the fact attendance is important.. that it sets you up for your life in the world of work but then I'd be telling my child it's more important to drag yourself to work than it is to look after yourself. So, we didn't.
>
> It feels a little bit wrong not to be supporting the school, or even to be directly going against them, but we've decided we won't be celebrating attendance awards and they won't be going on the fridge! I am just as concerned as their school when they miss learning time; being around their friends or the inevitable impact it has on us as parents when one of us has to take a day off work to look after them. I also understand that the school is judged on their attendance and find themselves between a rock and a hard place but there must be a better way to celebrate students than to issue awards for what essentially amounts to the roll of a dice.

> I think of all of the things my children have been rewarded for this year; excellent maths work; sports awards and reading challenges. I think of how happy they always are to receive them and show them to us and then of the opposite, of the child sat in an assembly hall whilst the vast majority of their peers walk up to receive an attendance certificate. I think that could be a pretty damaging experience – I know it was upsetting for my son.
>
> As parents we will always try to do what's best for our child – if that means not sending them to school when they are sick then that's what we will do. Should they be excluded from rewards for this? Hopefully you will reflect on this and consider all of the other amazing things our children do in schools each and every day of the year and realise that rewarding attendance is pretty low down on the scale.
>
> **John**

Questions to Ask of Yourself, Your Team, Your Staff, Your Students or Your Wider Community

What is the ultimate goal for attendance in this school in the long term?

Does our attendance policy meet the needs of our community and our local context?

Does what's written in our attendance policy translate into practise in the reality of the school day?

Is our attendance policy accessible to all member of our community? Are key messages communicated in different languages/simply enough?

Is our attendance policy created in isolation or do we consult key stakeholders in its creation?

How do we review our attendance policy and whether it is appropriate/meets our needs?

Are the consequences of poor attendance understood by all of the school community?

Are we clear on how to spot patterns likely leading to poor attendance and how staff should address it?

Do we communicate enough with our community around attendance and how do we ensure that the message stays fresh?

How do we/would we deal with concerns/suggestions raised around the use/implementation of the attendance policy?

How do we communicate changes to the attendance policy to our community and how do we ensure those changes have been heard?

How do we reward good attendance and how do we check that these rewards are valued by the children receiving them?

How do we ensure that our attendance policies and practises are inclusive for children with SEND or medical conditions?

Which external agencies do we work with to support student attendance? How often do we review these/look for other providers?

Do staff at all levels understand how attendance is calculated in schools and can they effectively advise/guide students/parents with this information?

How often do staff get the chance to see other schools/provisions to develop new ideas and observe best practise?

How often do we review the effectiveness of our attendance systems using data/evidence?

What do we report to parents? Are days missed, sessions missed or percentage absences more useful for our community?

8 Administration

One of the biggest changes to your working life when you move into a pastoral role is the influx/overload/existential nightmare that is the amount of emails/correspondence you receive. It's easy to forget something after you've read it, particularly if it is something small within a busy day, but somebody cared enough to send you that email, to talk to you about one of your year group or to invite you to a meeting/event. You will never be able to walk down a corridor again without somebody grabbing you, whether it's for a quick chat about Jacob in 10XY, to pop into a lesson or to support you with an issue.

In this chapter, I cover how to mitigate against those demands on your time, which quickly rack up and allow things to slip through the cracks. It's an obvious one but avoiding that is of utmost importance. Effective administration provides the consistency which I talk about a lot, and when we forget to do something or follow-up on an issue or problem, we start to erode that which is so necessary within our roles. This chapter provides tips and tricks on what to do to stay organised and to manage the mountain of paperwork that pastoral care provides!

Getting Organised

Different people will clearly organise themselves differently and in this section, I have collated a range of strategies, which are by no means exhaustive, which may help you stay organised. Some will contradict each other as we all have our own preferred ways of working – despite my computing degree, I have always leaned more on physical notation, reminders via post-its on the desk and things I actually see – this goes against everything you might expect of someone who loves technology. What is important is testing out what works for you and reflecting on your practise as a result

– I've settled firmly into a hybrid model of a balance of technology and physical administrative methods that I find works really well – this is a decision you need to make for yourself.

- Set up email folders and flag anything you haven't responded to – check these at the end of every day to check items you need to follow-up. There is accepted research that shows this has no real-time benefit but for some, it creates a level of organisation that provides some clarity and security.

- Get a small notebook for your pocket/person and a large notebook for when you are sitting in an office/base. If somebody stops you in the corridor with a task either get them to email it to you (if they aren't really bothered, trust me, it won't arrive) or write it into your small notebook. At the end of the day, transfer any tasks from that and your emails into the large notebook as a to-do-list for the next day. This can also be a good reflective tool to see where you are spending your time.

- Set up your diary early – whether it's electronic on your email system or a physical diary. I had both so that I could easily check if I was available while in a meeting or off-site but an electronic calendar, was shared with other people on the team, to check my availability (pastoral admin, etc.). I have previously worn a fitness band that reminds me of every element of my school day at this point and is linked to my Outlook calendar – I can't count how often that saved me from forgetting a calendared event.

- Keep on top of any admin you receive – you'll receive requests for all kinds of information about students, whether it's admissions information to/from new schools, external agencies requesting information or governor reports the list is huge and scrambling to fill them in last minute will make your life more difficult. Add deadlines into your calendar so that none of these can sneak up on you – I've had far too many "Oh no!" moments at midnight where I've remembered I haven't filled in a report for a meeting the next day.

- Make it clear to receptionists/admin staff how you would like parental concerns/feedback sent to you – one of my bugbears is an email with "John Smith's parent rang to speak to you and wants a call back" as it means I have to load the information system, look for the child, try ringing both parents, etc. Encourage staff to share with you the information you will need to make that call quickly – "John Smith's father rang, Mr Smith 07777 777 777, and would like a call back between 11am and 2pm if possible". It's a small thing but that time during the day adds up.

There are equally many ways of automating systems and software like Microsoft's Planner exist for you to add tasks/to-do lists for yourself and your teams which you can see added/ticked off live.

- Prepare for meetings ahead of time but make sure you have any information printed and checked before you take it into a meeting. You'll spend a lot of time meeting with parents in all likelihood so getting this process down from the start will help you in the long run as they will very often be keen to discuss information the school holds. The same goes for internal meetings with staff, governors, etc. Fail to prepare and prepare to fail, of course.

- You will be asked for information about students constantly. Whether that is by SLT, parents, colleagues or any other stakeholder who may need data. It is in your best interests to ensure that you are keeping accurate records of student information that you are responsible for from the very beginning – a Head of Year I used to work with would produce a year group folder at the start of the year with contextual information for the year group inside. It contained things like lists of pupils within particular groups (PP, SEND, EAL, CLA, etc.), records of meetings/minutes and the levels of each, support and intervention offered to students, behaviour/achievement/attendance/academic data. It's a great resource to refer to and will allow you to keep important information for your year group quickly at hand.

- If you are responsible for minuting meetings that you lead, then make sure they are typed up while it's still fresh in yours and other's memory in case anything needs to be clarified.

- If you are responsible for recording or analysing student data, then keep this organised whether that's in electronic or physical folders. Be clear about when data is recorded or run and where this comes from – ideally, you want to be in a situation where data is available for you at regular points and you don't need to request for it be created.

- If you are responsible for leading pastoral staff, do you reflect on the tasks you ask them to do, whether regular or irregular? There is nothing that frustrated me more than having five Heads of Year be given the same task, which could quite easily have been centralised/completed by one person. A prime example that would annoy me every time I had to do it was sending out a weekly schedule for tutor time activities to the tutor team. This was produced centrally and the expectation was that the HOY emailed it to their tutors – there was no difference between the year group activities. Instead of the person who created the timetable sending it out, they insisted each HOY sent it personally to their teams. This meant five separate people doing the same job, which could have been done by one. If your staff raise issues like this with you, that ultimately will save them time, then it's probably wise to look into it.

- On a similar level, ensure that the data staff need to do their job is shared in a timely, and most importantly, usable fashion. I have lost count of the number of times I have been asked to provide data support to a person/team where the formatting can be adapted and the data can be run off to show exactly what the person is looking for, rather than them having to interrogate it ten different ways. If you have a data expert in your school, trust or even in a school you network with then it would be a sensible idea to show them what you use/do and see if there are smarter ways to make use of that data. The admin time saved here can be huge – as a leader of a pastoral team/pastoral staff you should be keeping yourself apprised of developments with data/reporting as those staff with responsibility for day-to-day management of operational issues are unlikely to have the headspace to do so.

- If you have staff working for you/with you who have responsibilities for administration, then have a discussion with them about your expectations/desires for the things they produce. Often, staff will do what a previous line manager expected of them – I once worked with someone who produced a set of reports every week for a year before her new line manager realised that she was doing it – nobody knew they existed other than the previous line manager!

- Hopefully, you will get the opportunity for handovers with people who hold roles you are taking over. The quality and time afforded to these will vary but done well are an incredible resource for a new member of the pastoral team to tap into. Try and find out as much information as you can about the students/staff you will be working with, strategies that work in difficult situations/how to motivate particular pupils, information about tutors, any major moments that occurred in the previous year, useful historical information such as students who engage with external agencies. If you aren't able to have a handover (and I really would push for one unless the situation of the person leaving makes this difficult) then you can find a lot of this information out for yourself. Have reports run for all of the information above that's on your schools' systems such as the previous year's behaviour and attendance information.

Being Organised When It Comes to Others

We must also be aware of the flip side of administration and the role that we play in asking other staff to provide information/complete administrative tasks. Round robins, email circulars and requests for student information come at staff at a mile-a-minute in schools – whether it's for a pastoral meeting, a SEND review or any of the many meetings on our varied calendars – there is a lot of admin to do when it comes to keeping tabs on our students. All of the information-gathering procedures we send out are necessary, and often vital, in ensuring that we are reporting an accurate picture to any number of stakeholders including parents, social services, the police and many more. That doesn't change the fact that it's a tough task to keep up with sometimes for us and for the staff we collate information from.

We are often bound by the formats sent to us by external agencies when it comes to requesting that information so there isn't much we can do to help here as staff, unfortunately, just need to work within the boundaries given. What I would encourage you to do is to reflect on how you use the information gathered for internal meetings and how you collect that information. A lengthy document that tells you a great deal about a student might be really useful – but when the only ones you receive are from the long-suffering Mrs Jethwa in English, who always diligently fills them out perfectly in the 2-day window, are they doing the job you want? Would you be more successful asking for 3 strengths and 3 areas for improvement? Would a virtual form with drop-downs be easier for your staff to fill in? You need to ensure you either enforce the collection methods you use or adapt them to fit the needs of your staff.

Paying Close Attention to the Role of Data

Running alongside this is your school's data collection system for assessments and attitude to learning scores etc. As a pastoral leader how much influence do you have on this and the usefulness of the data which is collected? I worked in a school that collected 8 different scores against their 8 values – rate on a scale of 1–5 how kind the student has been in your lessons this half-term, how resilient they have been…it took an age to complete even one class and very quickly became a point of contention amongst staff. I'm sure in someone's head this was an excellent opportunity to see how well the school's values were being embedded across the school – the reality was that the data were not reliable as most staff copied and pasted column to column – if you teach a once per week subject you could be entering upwards of 300 sets of 8 scores per child, that is, 2400 separate pieces of data!

Once you are clear on the data you are collecting from staff and other internal/external sources it's important to look at how the data is used and where. Do the pastoral team all run meetings in the same way? It's a question worth asking to ensure that you aren't wasting teacher time. In a previous school, the pastoral admin team would send out a round-robin for every pastoral meeting and then pass these along to the Heads of Year. For some, these would be the centrepiece of the meeting and for others they were worth a cursory glance. I've sat in meetings before, reading round-robins that I've asked for, and reading out 2/8 responses that are half-way decent and thinking that most of the information isn't particularly useful. We must make sure if we ask for this information, we are using it in the best way possible so that we can report back to staff how it's used and offer thanks for the feedback.

Are Your Admin Systems Efficient?

There is equally a question to be asked about whether our processes for the management of areas linked to pastoral care utilise the correct amount of administration. Talk to staff in your schools about how they have observed the process of setting/recording detentions and you will no doubt be shocked at some of the practises which occur – or maybe you will be the one with the shocking experience. I've seen environments where when a student gets a detention the member of staff has to write out a detention slip on a carbon copy triplicate (one for the student, parents and staff issuing it) where they then have to log the detention on their tracking system, call parents, log if the student attended and then follow up if this isn't the case – as well as ensuring everyone gets their copy! Even the most well-intentioned staff don't have the time in their busy schedules to work within a system like that and the consequence is that staff have a reticence about handing out detentions as they know the workload that will come with it or that the data entered into your systems isn't an accurate reflection of the picture on the shop floor.

We need to ensure that our systems are as easy for staff to use/utilise as possible and that the impact on their workload is as slight as we can keep it – part of this process is in reflecting on what is the most important thing you need staff to be doing and ensuring that all of the other systems are able to take a backseat to it. It's also important to regularly put yourself into the shoes of your staff who are most exposed to changes to strategy/policy – it's easy to forget how you were impacted by onerous policies before you were responsible for them.

It's worth regularly reviewing the strategies/tools you use within your pastoral system to ensure that they are still fit for purpose – I have seen plenty of schools where systems are still in place because it's a difficult or time-consuming job to change them rather than because they are the best option for the school community – don't shy away from the difficult decisions if you know that the alternative is better for your school. With school budgets tightening at a rate of knots, it's important that we ensure our crucial administrative systems are as streamlined and effective as possible – ignore them at your peril!

Questions to Ask of Yourself, Your Team, Your Staff, Your Students or Your Wider Community

- What are the biggest 'time sink' tasks that I have to undertake daily? Weekly? Monthly?
- Is there any way for me to change the way I work to ensure that these do not take as much time?
- Have I spoken to other staff about how they manage these tasks and are there lessons to be learned from them?
- Am I clear and direct with how staff should raise concerns or issues with me – do I want these by email, by phone, face to face, etc.?
- Am I confident and comfortable in telling somebody I do not have time to do something or that I need more time to achieve it? Can I have this conversation before something becomes an issue?
- Do I know who I can ask for support if I'm struggling workload/time management – have I asked them if they would be happy to support with XYZ if needed?
- As a line manager, do I clearly offer my support to those who report to me and do I believe they are comfortable in asking for it? If not, why not?
- Does the school duplicate tasks/duties for different people/sources – can we streamline or remove tasks entirely if they are already done elsewhere/similarly?
- Do we use data sensibly and are the reports/information we use formatted/sourced in a manner that saves us time and allows us to interrogate data at an appropriate level?

Do I keep myself appraised of networking/collaborative opportunities where I can become aware of new strategies/developments in the field that can save time/improve efficiency?

Are there centralised systems that could be developed, or purchased, which would ease the administrative load on staff?

Have we looked at other schools and their systems for managing administrative tasks?

Are we using our administrative staff in the best manner possible – are there areas that are struggling or areas who could support?

9 Safeguarding

Ralph Waldo Emerson famously said, 'As soon as there is life, there is danger' and boy do you know it if you work in pastoral care. Safeguarding in schools is our single-most important role and as time progresses, it seems our role in this great behemoth is ever growing. Some would argue that there is more danger in the world than ever before – others would argue that we are just more aware of it. The litany of agencies we work with in schools, the devastating and depressing issues that land on our desks and the ever-developing online world all contribute to more safeguarding issues in schools than ever before.

When planning for this chapter, prior to writing, I half-considered writing a single message "Discuss any issues with the Designated Safeguarding Lead" as the most important piece of advice I could give – and if there is one thing more important than any other when it comes to safeguarding it is that. This doesn't however, provide you with the tools, skills or knowledge to feel comfortable within the world of safeguarding – to be honest, I'm not sure any book can. It is such an unpredictable and often punishing field to work within and there is nothing else like it. I thought instead it would be useful to fill this chapter with a number of real-life, anonymous examples of safeguarding issues so that you may get a feel for the realities of safeguarding and some of the actions taken which are all based around the reality of my own experiences; those I have worked with or from safeguarding reviews. What I do aim to do in this chapter is provide you with some practical advice and some common safeguarding issues you may come up against.

Always Be Prepared

First and foremost, you must prepare for situations where a safeguarding issue could swallow the next lesson, morning, day or even longer. The completely innocuous conversation or issue that you pick up can suddenly unravel into a complex and challenging safeguarding matter at a moment's notice. There is not much that you can actually do to prepare for this other than ensuring you have contingencies in place if you are suddenly taken away from a lesson, meeting, etc. This can be as simple as knowing who you will talk to for cover or having a go-to lesson to use at a pinch if needed.

You can also endeavour to ensure that the materials you need for reporting or dealing with safeguarding issues are always at the ready. I have had staff approach me in the past to report a safeguarding concern and, when asked to note it on an electronic system tell me they don't know their login details. Unfortunately for them, this doesn't absolve them of the need to log the incident and they are told to go and sort the problem out and then log it. Similarly, if you are responsible for investigating these incidents and there are forms that need to be filled in or systems that need to be followed, then ensure you have these at your disposal, ready to be used if needed.

Take Notes

Be methodical with your logging and recording of information during the entirety of the process. The nature of safeguarding is that, unfortunately, anything not recorded will likely come back to bite you. It is often the case that many of the safeguarding issues we deal with materialise at a later date in the form of a further issue, and having a detailed description of events will help you to familiarise yourself with previous events.

This also allows staff who take over responsibility for the safeguarding of students/groups, etc. the ability to back-track and build an understanding of safeguarding issues where necessary. Whilst all of the above is useful for us the other side of the coin with safeguarding is that any issue reported could later develop into a much wider problem. If you are the member of staff who reports a bruise on a student's face, this could, in two months, be used as evidence in court proceedings for the removal of a child from an abusive parent. If you have ever been trained as a Designated Safeguarding Lead, or you have any interest in the area, you will know that there have been serious failings in safeguarding by many authorities, including schools, which have resulted in the deaths of children.

You can find many serious case reviews on the internet that point to a lack of, or poor, recording of incidents, or sharing of those incidents with relevant professionals, which have contributed to these devastating consequences. Unfortunately, with public services being so clinically underfunded it is the case that our police, NHS, social services – like education – find themselves unable to deal with the rising number of safeguarding concerns that present in schools and the onus is on us to ensure that we are logging and recorded all of our concerns as clearly and quickly as possible.

Legal Implications and Considerations

There are phrases now prevalent within the world of safeguarding, "Professional Curiosity" and "Respectful Uncertainty", which sum up the role of anyone involved in dealing with safeguarding issues. To be clear, if a child is disclosing something to you and you are not a safeguarding lead, you should follow the guidance offered by your school, which will almost inevitably be to listen, not to ask questions or make judgements and to then report this to a DSL immediately.

If you are investigating safeguarding issues, professional curiosity is about exploring issues respectfully and not necessarily taking what you're told at face value. The child with the bruise on his face may well have fallen over at the weekend and banged it on the TV stand – you may never get any answer other than this from him or his parents. The fact remains, you need to be alert to the idea that this may not be the case. Criticisms in serious case reviews often refer to parents/carers who appear compliant or co-operative and, as a result, agencies involved backing off or reducing support, despite a developing picture that continues to cause concern.

I have myself experienced a set of parents who, whenever social services or the school would visit, would ensure that food was in the cupboards and the children had been taken elsewhere to shower and clean. The reality of this situation was that, in between visits, there was very often no food in the house and the facilities were barely usable. The children, despite the dire situation they found themselves in, had been coached that if they did not conform to the story they would be taken away by social services, moved schools and split up from their siblings. This is why we must always be professionally curious and involve external agencies as early as we can to ensure that the children we care for are safe and healthy.

Clarity and Rigour

As a pastoral/school leader, it is our utmost responsibility to ensure that our safeguarding policies/procedures are robust and clear. It is our duty to ensure that we overcommunicate these with our students; our staff; our parents and our governors so that every member of our community knows what to do when a situation arises. As time-consuming and draining as dealing with safeguarding issues is, I would much rather we found ourselves in the position of having 100% of incidents reported than having members of our community unsure of how to, or whether they should, report incidents.

Safeguarding issues arise from every facet of our school lives – a conversation with a parent; an overheard conversation; some graffiti on a wall, or the smell of alcohol on someone's breath. We must be alert to every eventuality and remember that the phrase 'It couldn't happen here' or 'That doesn't happen here' most likely just means you don't know that it already is.

Taking Care of Yourself

My final word on safeguarding prior to commencing with the case studies is this – look after yourself and those around you. Anybody who works within pastoral care/safeguarding knows the immense drain that comes with dealing with safeguarding issues, or experiencing them as a student, some of which will have been unimaginable for you before doing so. Good supervision, somebody to offload confidentially to, makes all the difference here – don't feel like you need to carry that weight on your shoulders.

You are responsible for the well-being of many within your care but it is just as important to take time for yourself – it's easy to dwell on things that have happened at work in a pastoral care role, and you need to have the tools/mechanisms at your disposal to let go. Thinking about a child who has been taken into care on the Friday evening; the child you know is sitting next to a parent's hospital bed or the child returning home to a house with no heating are all huge, real concerns but those children may need your support in school and you can't offer that if you've broken yourself down.

Take the time to relax at home and unwind – make sure that you are the rested and energetic version of you that can really make a difference to their lives by ensuring that you take down-time as often as you can – enjoy hobbies, take time with family and friends, and generally just ensure that you do things that make you happy.

> ### Case Study 9.1 Reflecting on Real World Examples
>
> You will find below some fictionalised, but very common, examples of safeguarding concerns which you will come across working within pastoral care. In them, I have drawn from examples from my own career

which I have either been a part of, read about or observed from the work of others. I would encourage you to read them and reflect with me on whether the approach taken was effective and whether you would do anything differently. Across the country, and the world, we all have different safeguarding systems within our settings and so your reflections may be different to others.

Child A – Taking Great Care to Remain Professionally Curious

Child A had been coming into school on an irregular basis and when he did arrive he looked tired, dishevelled and was more irritable than previously experienced. His already challenging behaviour was becoming unmanageable. In conversations with his parents, they claimed this was due to the fact he was staying out until all hours of the evening and that they could not control him. In reality, his father had been getting increasingly physical as a means to control his son's behaviour – to no avail. This had culminated one evening in father and son having a stand-up fight in the house and the child being kicked out. The story told to the school eventually was that the child had assaulted the father who had kicked him out and rendered him homeless and that they didn't care where he ended up. The police and social services at this point became involved but only to clarify to the father that he could not abdicate responsibility for his son and that he needed to either allow him to return or find alternate living arrangements for him with family/friends. Ultimately, he ended up 'sofa-surfing' for a period of time. The reality of the situation still hadn't been realised until it was discovered that the child's behaviour had been deteriorating due to being influenced by a local drugs gang who had been using him to deal drugs in the evening.

Reflections

This story doesn't have a particularly happy ending and is not one that illustrates exemplary practise – there was more that could be done at all levels to discover the true picture of what was happening with this child. It does however further push home the idea that we need to remain professionally curious – in this situation school staff, police and social services were all spun different stories by the parties involved and, ultimately, it meant the prolonged exposure of a child to drug gangs. In this example, whilst staff were aware of problem A (the issues in the home) they did not have any awareness of problem B (the drug dealing) which was causing the overall problem. One of the agencies involved was aware of this but had not communicated it to the school - it is a lesson in not making assumptions and working together to best safeguard children.

Child B

Child B had been taking inappropriate pictures of themselves and sending these to a variety of strangers of varying ages online. A student in school reported this to a member of staff having been made aware of the fact that other students in the school had some of these pictures on their phone. The school investigation was long and drawn out – eventually lasting for a period of months as the images cropped up in different places and via different students – even extending to other schools. Throughout the process, various external agencies had become involved including social services and the police. The initial investigation involved senior designated safeguarding leads in the school and was led by a single individual to preserve a continuous understanding of the multiple branches the investigation took. The social services and police involvement reached senior levels as it became clear that there was an element of grooming involved, perhaps by an adult. The investigation ultimately hinged on the initial work/statements taken at the beginning of the investigation – on day one. Child B had shared relatively little information and had initially told a story that bore no resemblance to the facts later known – the diligence of the pastoral staff investigating had ensured that, with the advice of the police, appropriate questions had been asked. As the pastoral staff had been trained on how to investigate incidents of potential sexual abuse, and had a wider knowledge of social media and applications used for communication, they were able to develop an understanding of the realities of the situation. Had they not known the intricacies of social media; Snapchat and WhatsApp then much of the original information provided by the student may have been taken at face value.

Reflections

This case study is a cautionary tale – the excellent work done by pastoral staff here ultimately protected a child from exploitation. Much of the success of the team was down to specialist knowledge and having an appraisal of the apps, software and devices students use. **This case highlighted the need for specific, relevant and up-to-date training from experts on apps and tools being used to communicate by students – it shows the importance of remaining up-to-date with the technology students are accessing and, if we reflect on what could have happened if the member of staff was not aware of the apps being used, the dire consequences that could have occurred.**

Child C – The Necessity of Regularly Reviewing Safeguarding Procedures

Child C absconded from school, having arrived early in the morning, prior to registration. The school policy and procedure is that an absence text goes to parent/carer at 9:30 am to inform them that their child is not in school

– this is then followed by a call from a member of staff if there is no response/acknowledgement from the parent/carer. On the day that Child C absconded from school, staff capacity/absence, meant that this message did not go out until later in the day and the parent was unaware their child was not in school. This resulted in the parent reporting their child as missing to the police who, after a day of searching, found them safe and well. The school missed a critical window for establishing whether Child C should have been in school – there were policies and procedures in place to ensure that any child not in school would have this communicated home. The system fell down however due to an extenuating circumstance – is this appropriate with regards to safeguarding children? As a member of pastoral staff, or safeguarding staff, we have a duty to protect the children within our care. It isn't good enough to assume that systems/procedures do that job for us without regular review.

Reflections

How often are safeguarding procedures, or in this case a wider safeguarding procedure in attendance management, reviewed within your school/trust? Staffing changes; changes to expectations/working arrangements; staff capacity and more can all have an impact on whether a policy is enacted. I would encourage you to think of all of the policies/procedures within your school which, if they fail, would result in a child not being safeguarded appropriately. Undertake an exercise to try and pick holes in the systems – check that you truly understand how they operate – we are all guilty of assuming a system that we put into place a couple of years ago still functions and runs exactly as saw it doing then, the reality is that this may not be the case. *It is very often a useful exercise to conduct a pre-mortem when thinking of new systems, or reviewing current ones. Begin with the idea that the system has failed – what is the worst case scenario that could have occurred? As a team, you must then discuss how this happened. This allows for an approach centred around radical candor – there has been no failing and nobody is to blame but you are establishing what may happen in the worst-case scenario and working backwards on how you would ensure it doesn't happen again. This then allows you to build those safeguards into your current policy and practice.*

Child D – Practising Persistence

Child D had spent much of Year 7 at home with an increasingly poor attendance record. The family were known to social services and Early Help had been offered and refused due to the parent's distrust of the social care system. On entry to Year 8 one of the pastoral team managed to convince the student into school by moving them into the nurture group. This was a great success and the student flourished in school. Unfortunately, the parent's own mental health issues brought allegations that the school were causing depression in Child D and that she would come home from school stressed and would self-harm – there was no evidence of this and this was confirmed by social services. The parent grew increasingly more erratic and would ring the school threatening to call the police as they had kidnapped her daughter; lost her or were abusing her. She would tell social services that the student did not eat and had an eating disorder – in school the student would eat well and would report having little to no food available at home. At each stage of this process, the staff logged the differing pictures experienced on the school safeguarding system. Eventually, the social services interventions stopped and the parent reverted to keeping Child D away from school – staff conducted home visits and reported further issues to social services to no avail. Staff responsible for safeguarding in the school shared their clear concerns with social services that this was a child in need of serious support. Professional curiosity in the staff continued to be of great importance and they eventually wrote a letter of complaint to the social services team stressing the many concerns observed and outlined and the fact that the school's position was not being listened to – there had also been an allegation within the household that one of the children had been physically assaulted. When sharing with social services that the school felt that Child D displayed many traits of a child being abused support was still not offered. Finally, a disclosure was made by a sibling to their school and a strategy meeting was arranged with the police to which Child D's school were not invited. Again, the school staff found themselves on the outside trying to push their way in. The culmination of this case study is that Child D disclosed similar issues to the police when interviewed and the school had the records of every conversation/letter to social services asking for support/intervention – school staff knew something was wrong and did not take the word of the external agencies involved but continued to prioritise their safeguarding policies with regard to Child D.

Reflections

This is a cautionary real-life example to show that as school staff you must exercise your safeguarding duties even when other agencies involved seem uninterested or advise otherwise. This also applies when external agencies are on site – ensure you are familiar with other elements of safeguarding practise that may impact you like the law around appropriate adults for police interviews; the Department for Educations Searching, Screening and Confiscation Policy or how legislation like The Human Rights Acts or Rights to Privacy apply in schools. **As a safeguarding** *professional you have a duty to be strong and to consider the rights and protection of the children in your care... even when it may mean butting heads with other agencies. Always log these communications/complaints and escalate to relevant managerial staff wherever needed. Early in my career an independent Chair of a social care panel proved to be particularly difficult, citing any challenge to social care as inappropriate. Fundamentally, social services were failing in their support for the child involved and this challenge needed to occur. Ultimately, it was escalated above both myself and the Chair and the child received the support they needed – it was an uncomfortable situation but one which needed to be addressed.*

School A – Addressing Culture Issues

School A found that increasingly safeguarding issues were going unreported and that students had bowed to a culture of not being a 'snitch' or 'grass'. Staff would regularly pick up an issue at its climax or after the worst had happened and then would have to pick up the pieces. Through reviewing this and the pastoral/safeguarding staff raising this as a concern it was decided that a concerted effort needed to be made to break the idea that raising a concern or discussing an issue was inherently bad or that it was disloyal to their peers. They ran a series of assemblies; developed tutor time materials and brought in external speakers on a range of issues that were impacting the school community. This included speakers discussing gang activity; the police; domestic violence and more. The consistent message that they asked all of the speakers to push was the idea that 'If you see something, say something' and they impressed upon students, with clear examples from their community and the wider world, the impact that stopping a safeguarding issue before it develops could have on others. They also ensured there were multiple ways to report issues so that students could speak to specific staff if needed; contact an email address or drop a concern in a box checked every hour. They would regularly refer to the idea in an effort to build this shared language within their community and to drive the idea that to protect others we need to share information.

Reflections

This clear focus on a specific issue drove safeguarding referrals up and students became more confident in reporting issues to staff. The school were clear – with safeguarding referrals up they could have a much better impact in their community and strive to work with students to solve problems before they arose. *Sometimes we need to look at incidents alone and other times they are reflective of wider community issues – in dealing with safeguarding*

> concerns you must have an awareness of this and respond accordingly. Diagnosing the correct problem is important within safeguarding and oftentimes we are drawn to the immediacy of solving an issue for an individual which makes it harder for us to see the bigger picture – this is where it is important to ensure that you can reflect, be that with your manager/team or during supervision, and identify whether problems you have identified are a bigger issue within your community.

A Final Word

The case studies above are examples of incidents that will be arising in our schools on a more regular basis than you may expect– we will never eradicate safeguarding issues; all we can hope to do is ensure that our systems and procedures are fit for purpose and that they meet the needs of our communities. A safeguarding concern/referral is not a failure of a school – it is a failure of a school if that referral/concern is not addressed or appropriately dealt with. We are all human and none of us are infallible – the key takeaway here is to reflect on our practise and, when we do get it wrong, ensure that we take every mitigation to ensure that it does not happen again.

Questions to Ask of Yourself, Your Team, Your Staff, Your Students or Your Wider Community

- Have you had any serious safeguarding incidents, or minor specialist incidents, in which an individual or team has developed knowledge which, if shared, could develop the skillset of your other pastoral staff?
- Are you, and all of your staff, aware of their statutory duties in relation to safeguarding – how do you know?
- What would a visitor to the school hear if they asked your students/staff/community about safeguarding and its effectiveness in your school?
- Are all staff aware of the signs that a young person may be suffering from a type of abuse, neglect or harm?
- Who is trained as a deputy designated safeguarding lead in your school – what is the rationale for this?

- Is our safeguarding policy regularly reviewed, in line with statutory guidance? Who is responsible for this and for quality assuring that all elements are in place?
- Do you have a good understanding of the contextual safeguarding issues which affect your community?
- Do you engage with external agencies to keep track of these, e.g., can your local policing team provide information about criminality amongst young people in the local area?
- How do you keep pastoral staff, and staff, appraised of the most up-to-date dangers to children? These may not be items covered in annual safeguarding training – think about uses of specific language or organisations which may be a risk to children. For example, would your staff be able to identify language linked to incel culture or AI and would they understand associated risks?
- Do you have a restraint or physical intervention policy – is this regularly reviewed with your safeguarding policy? If yes, how do you know that instances of physical restraint have been logged and followed up on in a timely and appropriate manner?
- How often is safeguarding practise reviewed/quality assured – are specific incidents looked into in greater deal as part of reflective practise to see if there would have been different ways to approach similar incidents in future?
- Have you considered supervision opportunities for pastoral staff exposed to serious safeguarding issues to protect their mental health/wellbeing and encourage reflective practise?
- Are staff aware of who to contact in specific scenarios such as a safeguarding concern raised against a member of staff?

10 Working with Parents and Carers

Parent/carer communication is easy to get right, painful when you get it wrong and downright disastrous if it goes really wrong. It's sometimes easy to forget that when we speak to parents, or communicate via other means, that the person on the other end of the line is also a living, breathing human with their own worries and concerns as well as their own day job or personal life to manage. It's also easy to forget how you desire to be spoken to when you are ringing a parent, period five on a Friday, after their darling child has thrown gluesticks at your ceiling in a lesson and one dropped and landed in Chelsea's newly done-up bun.

You want to get your point across, tell the parent what their child has done wrong, alongside any sanction, and get out of there as quickly as possible. Unfortunately, in doing so, you set yourself up to fail and the building blocks for a poor parental relationship begin to stack on top of each other. You'll soon realise that once the blocks have started to stack, each conversation you have results in them stacking faster, to the point you dread ringing Mr Smith at all because you know how the conversation will go.

In this chapter, I discuss the power of parental partnerships and how, as pastoral staff, we can build strong and effective relationships with parents/carers. Oftentimes these relationships are the lynchpin of improving student attitudes, behaviour, attendance, etc. and you must focus on developing your skills to ensure that you can cultivate strong relationships within the community you serve.

It's An Open Road

In reality, there really aren't many occasions where a parental phone call should be challenging – a difficult conversation may need to be had but that doesn't mean that it needs to be one which results in either party leaving it and feeling like they've done 12 rounds with Mike Tyson.

As a Pastoral Leader there are some incredibly difficult conversations to be had; you may find you need to end a conversation and pick it up later; or times when the 5-minute phone call becomes 30 mins-1 hr of trying to resolve a multitude of issues; or times when you need to hang up and had to call social services or the police.

You never know where a phone call home, or a chat on the gate, or any other method of communication might take you. You should know, however, that there are some really simple things you can do to make sure that parental communication/relationships needn't be the bogeyman.

The Fine Art of Communication

Parental communication, and by extension co-operation, is one of the biggest keys to your success as a mentor, TA, Teacher, Pastoral Leader, etc. Most parents will want to work with you to ensure their child's school life is the best it can possibly be – almost all parents will want to ensure their child's school life is the best it can possibly be but may not want to work with you!

Courtesy and respect go a long way in building strong working relationships with parents – the vast majority of your communications with parents will likely be by phone. I can't count the number of times I've sat with a member of staff who starts a phone call to a parent with "Hello, it's Mr X from school, John was a nightmare in his DT lesson today". Those kinds of opening messages get most parent's backs up straight away – don't do it. Introduce yourself, start by asking them if they are alright, if they have a couple of minutes to talk and you'll often find they are much more willing to engage with you. That's not always the case but if you've taken the time to be respectful at the start of the conversation, you will have at least set the table for a polite conversation. Think about how you feel when the insurance salesman rings at 6 pm, after a long day, and asks you if you've got some time to talk – I'm certainly not comparing us to cold callers but for some parents the feeling is the same!

Try and ensure that your first communication with a parent isn't a negative one wherever possible – when we take over a class/group, or first start working with a child, we generally know where we might expect problems. Get early conversations in with their parents by spotting praise where possible within the first few interactions you have with their child – this will make it easier for you to call later on if you need to ring for less positive reasons.

"What's he done now?" is one of the most common responses I receive when calling a parent/carer. For some of our communities the thought of a telling off from school brings back negative memories of their own and this is always something to be cognizant of. Even if you can't see any opportunities for praise you can still call and introduce yourself in situations where you feel it may be beneficial – if you take over a class, for example, that you know have been historically poorly behaved there's no harm in ringing some parents of key students to introduce yourself, acknowledge the issues from the past and then let them know you are going to be working to move things forward. You may even find that a parent/carer has suggestions/advice to offer that could be valuable for you, having never worked with their child before. I noted in the behaviour management section to 'Sweat the Small Stuff' and this extends to praise and reward for those students where this may be few and far between.

Praise phone calls, postcards, emails, etc. will always be a great way to endear yourself to most parents/carers and you should endeavour to do this as much as you reasonably can. I've always been a fan of the 'Friday Five' approach – making five positive phone calls on a Friday – to end the week on a high and make five children's (and their parent's) weekends.

Keeping It Simple

Keep any reporting of behaviour as factual and clear as possible and, if you need to, think beforehand about the message you wish to convey. It can be hard for a parent to hear a statement like "Harry was incredibly rude, and his language was disgusting in the lesson" – you are much better off keeping it to what actually happened "Harry came into the classroom today and when I asked him to take off his coat, he told me to shut up" is harder hitting, much more accurate and also makes it sound less like it's your opinion.

When you report any sanctions you gave you may also want to link it clearly to the school's behaviour policy – "I had no choice but to have him removed in line with the school's behaviour policy and the sanction for that is a 1 hour detention" – this takes away some of the feeling that you are directly responsible for the sanction, and thus the person to direct any negative energy towards. If the time is right you can then start to talk about how to move forward, what your expectations for the student are and what the next lesson or interaction with them might look like. That is the ultimate goal – how can you improve the situation moving forward?

Always try to be aware of the time of day and the time your conversation may take – if you know you need to have a long chat with a parent don't just call and expect them to drop everything for you – there's nothing wrong with letting them know this could be a longer conversation and asking if there's a more convenient time for them. Equally, in reverse, you aren't obligated to take a call that sucks up all of your precious time and you need to be willing to do the same thing for yourself.

The more you get to know certain parents, the more you will know their working patterns and their ability to talk with you. Share this information with pastoral staff if you develop it so that other members of staff can benefit from what you've found. Some parents will prefer email communication due to their availability and if this works for you it can be a really powerful way to address concerns that also removes some of the emotion brought by a phone call – all I would say is to treat it as you would an internal email – keep it professional and respond within your working hours.

It's also important to make sure that you are aware of who you are calling, and their relationship to the child, and make every effort possible to use the parent/carer's name. A pet hate of mine is "Is this Abby's mum?" – you should be using their name – in what other profession would you start a conversation like that?

It's OK to Delay

Be confident in ending a call, or meeting, if it does become problematic – there are some parents/carers who just won't countenance what you have to say – this may also stretch to abusive language or threats. This can be for any number of reasons but ultimately you do not come to work to be verbally abused. If you can feel a conversation is getting heated, then you are probably best to draw it to a close with a more definite statement "I'm hopeful that we can work together to achieve the best for XYZ but I think it's best if we pick this up again at a later date. Either I, or XYZ, will give you a call back in the next X days – thank you for your time". You can then decide if you need to escalate the conversation up the chain and get a more senior member of staff to call to resolve the issue, or whether some breathing room and time to digest the issue will mean you can have the conversation yourself at a later date.

It's always worth flagging this as an issue to your pastoral team, faculty or SLT as you may not be the only member of staff being put in this situation. For some staff, communication at home is something that brings anxiety and fear – this shouldn't be the case. I can count on one hand the number of phone calls home that I've made where I've ended the call feeling like it was unpleasant.

If you stick to some of the tried and tested approaches discussed here you should be able to develop a script and a methodology for communication that ensures that you always start off on the right foot and, when you don't, you know how to bring it to a conclusion. As with anything – the more you do the easier it becomes – for the past however many years I have started every phone call the exact same way (introduction, how are you, have you got time to talk?) and I doubt I'll ever change that now.

One final tip is to ask a member of staff who you know is regularly in touch with parents if you can shadow them making a couple of difficult calls, particularly to those you may have struggled with, and you'll soon see that it's a skill to be honed.

Case Study 10.1 Community Cohesion… Reaching Out to All Those Who form the Fabric of Your Students' Lives'

by Ed Finch
Primary School Teacher

In the COVID-19 lockdown of 2020, schools and their leaders faced a bewildering range of challenges. They didn't just worry about providing some continuity of education to their pupils who were at home, good leaders also broadened their gaze and asked themselves how they could support their communities. Through this work leaders came to see their relationship to those people they served very differently and, while this is not long in the past, we're starting to see that some of these changes might bear long-term fruit.

Adam Hill, a headteacher at Dartmoor Multi Academy Trust, found this experience of servant leadership ultimately enriching for the children at the schools he leads. Adam told me how, as soon as lockdown was announced, he started to reflect on the challenges for other people in the remote villages of west Devon. With what few civic spaces these rural communities have closed down, and travel reduced to a minimum, Adam swiftly realised that it was the youngest and the oldest members of the community that were most affected, those of working age could be using social media to stay in contact with friendship networks and might have work as a distraction – even if working remotely from home – but children and the elderly were genuinely isolated. For people already at risk of social isolation, lockdown magnified the risk hundreds of times.

Adam organised for the children of his school, both those in key worker groups at school and those learning from home, to discuss their responsibility to the elderly in their communities. To their credit, Adam told me, "We spoke to the children about it, and they were really empathetic – the children really got it and wanted to help which was great". Children made cards with messages of hope and then coordinated with networks that reach across communities to deliver them to the elderly and isolated – the local shop put the children's cards in with food deliveries, the church warden delivered them on his doorstep visits, many were distributed through old folks' homes and sheltered accommodation. And, somewhat to his surprise, Adam found that some of the recipients responded and wrote back to the young people of the school forging new links where none had been before.

Adam's schools, like so many others across the country, were delivering food parcels to families who would normally receive free school meals. The schools' leadership, thinking about the risks of isolation decided to think more widely and drew on charitable funds so they could widen this offer. They were able to make deliveries to families who might not be in receipt of free school meals but who, they knew, were struggling. Each week the school staff would create parcels and drive out to deliver them stopping at each house to have a genuine conversation with the recipients – not just checking they had food but creating opportunities for deeper conversations about wellbeing and also the opportunity for what might be the only social contact these people might be having from week to week. These conversations weren't just useful in themselves; the team found they were in a position to refer people for help or to signpost to services – they were reaching out into the community in a way they had never done before. Adam, and the teachers at the schools came to understand that, to many in their communities, the fact that schools were still open and that children were still learning in them was a real sign of positivity and hope at a time when everything else in these villages seemed to have come to a standstill. Together they decided to make this continuity more apparent to the people community. A changing display of photographs and messages was placed at the front of the school so people passing by could see that there really was still life, and hope, in their village.

Later into lockdown when, for a period, places of worship were allowed to open for private prayer, the school created displays of the children's writing and artwork so that visitors to the church could see the continuity of hope in the

> heart of the community. Through actions like these schools across the country found ways to link civic responsibility and relationships to their communities at the core of their mission. While it is early days yet Adam believes that the schools have been strengthened and relationships enriched by this. Movingly, Adam told me about an elderly man in one of the villages who, affected by dementia, finds it hard to relate to the world or to people around him and who, as a result had been regarded warily by the children of the school when he passed on his daily exercise. This gentleman received one of the cards the children had made and was, his wife said, deeply moved by it. The children, learning that the card had reached him and made such an impression started to look out for him as he passed on his daily walk with his wife and developed a habit of greeting him respectfully over the school wall each day. Some days he is able to respond, other days his condition is such that he cannot, but the habit has continued and enriches both the man and his wife and the children.
>
> Through service and through creativity in adversity it does seem that schools have been able to build more resilient and more meaningful relationships within their communities and this is a lesson that we should all perhaps continue to learn from.

Pros and Cons of Different Methodologies

There are many other ways of communicating with parents, other than speaking via telephone or face-to-face, for us to ensure that we get right as pastoral staff all of which contribute to a school that is valued by it's community and trusted by parents/carers. Consider all of the approaches you take to parental communication and make sure you are regularly taking feedback from the community as to whether they achieve the purpose they have been designed for.

Using School/Parent Apps

One example from my own work is a reflection on the move that a lot of schools are taking to develop/design apps that allow communication with parents; sharing of student timetables, achievements, behaviour and attendance; reporting, etc. This is a fantastic idea which, when done right, becomes a one-stop-shop for all things school for that parent and their children.

Report an absence? Do it on the app. Load lunch money? Do it on the app. Contact your child's tutor? Do it on the app. Great! The reality of getting all of that to work is tough and depends upon parental communication – that's right – to get parental communication right you need to communicate well with parents – ground-breaking, I know. What I mean by that is that I have seen this exact scenario, an app is launched, and the messages the school sends go as unread notifications; the reporting functionality brings more questions than answers; glitches/issues dominate the use of it. Before you know it, you are further away from outstanding parental communication than when you started.

This isn't to say that you shouldn't do it – like I said it's a fantastic idea when done right – but more of a caution to ensure that you don't walk before you can run. The last thing you want is angry parents knocking down the doors to reception because all of the much-promised features of an app aren't working.

Consult carefully with your stakeholders – what are the features they would most like to see? Prioritise these and get some functionality in place. Ensure that your student's parents have a keen understanding of separate, smaller elements of an app before launching multi-faceted, all-encompassing toolkits.

Benefits of Letters Home

Another method of communication that is slowly disappearing is the written letter, posted home or given out to students. Rightly, in a world where climate change and environmentalism should be taking centre stage and we should be moving to a paperless society. The issue here is that physical letters very often do a good job of getting a message to a wide number of parents – some will say that they never make it to the right parents or are thrown away before anyone has a chance to read them. I would challenge that and say what do you do as a school to mitigate this? Are parents aware that reports are coming home on XXX date and will be given to their child? Well, if so they are much more likely to receive it from their child if they know their parent is going to ask the question of where it is.

Equally, do you make the same point to students in school – "Your parents have all been informed that you are bringing reports home today." ensures that the vast majority of those reports will, indeed, make it home.

Note to Self: Remember to Use Accessible Language

One issue with letters (or any communication), whether electronic or printed, is ensuring that they meet the needs of the community that you serve. I was astonished to read a letter from a school whilst doing some due diligence for a job which, in a very heavily EAL community, could have been written by Shakespeare himself. The Headteacher, I'm sure was very educated and proud of their ability to present in prose but would the fairly essential messages they were trying to communicate be easily discernible by their community? I wasn't sure. In my current and previous schools, I have had parents outright tell me that they struggle to read/write and this is something I consider in every communication we make – how can I ensure that the message I need to get across is the most easily accessible for every member of the community?

There is no guarantee that someone who struggles to read will have someone with them to read the letter, or that they will even feel confident enough to ask someone, just as there is no guarantee that an EAL parent will be easily able to translate any communication sent from school. Only you know the needs of your community and you need to ensure that your communications don't alienate those who are most likely to already be alienated.

Lots of schools now have a dedicated 'letters' section on their website, which contains all non-specific communications home to parents – again a good idea if regularly maintained. I have worked in a school where letters are added a month after they are sent – not particularly useful. One of the advantages of this is that, with the right formatting, you can ensure that translate/language features such as auto-readers can be turned on for those parents who may struggle. Don't just assume that parents will know this however – you might need to call and show them how to so – the time investment will be returned in the end when you have members of your community far more able to engage and invest.

Websites and Their Uses

Whilst on the topic of school websites they, much like all websites, are quite varied across the sector. This is no criticism of individual schools – it's much easier for a school in a large trust to have a shiny, uniform website that is all singing/dancing in comparison with a tiny, village school. That doesn't, however mean that you can't still have a website that effectively supports your mission for excellent parental communication.

The cost to design/develop websites can be prohibitive in a world where school funding is already stretched – if that sounds like your school, then I'd still encourage you to try and budget for a website that really sells your school as it's often the first thing people see when they search for you. In the interim, if you have a more dated or difficult-to-use website, it's wise to limit what's on it to just those essential elements that parents need to see – alongside the elements that are required on your website as part of statutory guidance.

Ensure that you have someone looking at the data behind it – that wonderful new blog you have launched, which takes up staff time might only be getting two views a month – is it worth it? If you think it is then perhaps you need to look again at how you've communicated to parents that it exists and how easy it is to navigate.

This is something aimed specifically for school leaders as, as a member of pastoral staff, you are unlikely to have access to this kind of data but it's worth asking the question. If nobody visits the letters page on your website, or the class activities page or downloads your newsletters then it's worth looking at whether something needs to change – ultimately we don't have the time in schools to spend on activities that aren't productive, particularly when that time may be better focused elsewhere. Always remember though – what worked in one school for communicating with parents, may not work in another and vice-versa.

Parent/Carer Evenings

As a member of the pastoral team, you will no doubt have involvement with these, often yearly, touchpoints for parents and carers. Increasing attendance at parents' evenings is a key driver for improving communication at lots of schools and a good parents' evening can have a very positive impact on how parents/carers feel about communication in your school. The ever-difficult issue with parents' evenings is that often we do not see the parents we want to – sometimes this is exacerbated by different groups. It is worth considering whether you can offer different events or timeslots for harder-to-reach groups – I have seen success with SEND or PP coffee mornings, specific individual meetings for those parents we want to see the most and also with strategies such as ringing and setting up appointments for key parents before the booking window opens; calling and checking that parents have received communication on the dates for parents evenings at the start of the year, etc.

Dealing with Challenging School/Parent Situations

One final point I would touch on is how to repair damaged relationships with parents who are proving to be challenging, for any number of reasons. You may be surprised to learn that many schools have a number of parents banned from the premises due to their behaviour or communication either on or off-site. It's very unlikely that you will ever be able to 'fix' this kind of relationship and it's best to follow your school policies on communication.

When I was 19, I was based in the school reception whilst working as Cover Manager and would very often be exposed to the hustle and bustle of the school day. One particularly eventful morning a parent came storming into school demanding to speak to her child's Head of Year – there were four of us in reception, and unfortunately, this was a fairly regular occurrence – we didn't think anything of it. The Head of Year would come down and diffuse the situation and the parent would leave happy. On this occasion, however the parent, in the meeting room opposite reception, backed the Head of Year into a corner and began to push and assault them. Fortunately, whenever we thought a parent may be angry/upset we always ensured that the meeting room was observable and we were able to jump into action. I had to barge through the door, blocked by the parent, to create space for the Head of Year to leave and waited in the room with them until Senior Staff took over. The police arrived and arrested the parent and the next time I saw her was giving evidence in court – she was charged and, amongst other sanctions, ordered not to set foot near the school premises.

The only thing I could feel at the end of the ordeal was sadness that at the end of the day, a child had a parent so challenging that they could legally not visit her school. I give this example because there will inevitably be someone reading this who believes that labelling a parent as 'challenging' is unfair – in most scenarios this is probably true but there are occasions in which school staff are exposed to behaviours such as the above, criminal behaviours, for which there should be no level of tolerance or support.

In reality, when I refer to parents who are exhibiting challenging behaviours, I am referring to those who have lost trust for the school or who have had previously damaging relationships with staff. They will challenge assertions from staff; records of events or reports because they have lost faith in actions undertaken by the school. Repairing these relationships is hard and it often depends upon a concerted effort from the school to 'walk the talk' and ensure that any promises are delivered upon. I very often sit in meetings with parents in this position who will quote chapter and verse of things that they were told would happen for their child and, for whatever reason, didn't.

Ultimately, the best way to start afresh is to call this out with those parents and be clear that whilst you can only apologise for any previous perceived failures, that you will do everything you can to prove that the school wants to work with them and achieve the best for their child. Sometimes this will mean you need to spend longer explaining your decisions to these specific parents; you may need to be more explicit in showing how you are supporting their child or you might be best served just checking in on how they feel things are going with school. Whatever you do, just make sure that if you say you are going to do something that you either do it, or explain why you can't.

Having parents on your side is one of the greatest tools to have in your toolkit – the knowledge that you and their parents are working in sync is one that strikes fear into the hearts of many a troublemaker and can inspire many students to show their best self. It's an opportunity to be capitalised upon and one that can have a significant impact on the culture and success of your role/school/community.

> **Case Study 10.2 The Fence on the Edge of the Cliff**
>
> by Connor Thompson
> Head of Year
>
> As a pastoral leader, it is fair to say you are on the front line when dealing with parents, carers and family members. This, of course, is a good part of the job when working with them when they are supportive but there are times when you have to 'hold your nerve' and deal with the challenging conversations.
>
> Tom Bennett, in his book Running the Room, says "the teacher-student relationship is important, but it is built on trust - and trust is built on mutually predictable behaviour." This rings true in the role as you will have to meet parents or carers who feel their child doesn't deserve a detention, or a referral to isolation or even an exclusion. What you have to achieve is consistency that parents and carers know exactly what will happen. If you start removing these, then there is a chink in the armour for you and colleagues and this will be exploited in the future – no matter how harmless you feel it is now.
>
> Now it certainly isn't easy, I have been in rooms where parents and carers have become irate, raised their voice, started shouting, swearing, threatened to make formal complaints, refuse to speak to you in the future, move schools or refuse to come back, go to the Local Authority and even the police! You have got to remember you are talking about their child and of course they will defend. However, if you have all the information there and it is in policy, then you have to maintain the stance you are upholding because if you let them off, you let them down. I am also afraid there are occasions where the 'good students' get caught up and the easy option would be to think 'they're a good kid, it's alright to let them off.' That is where inconsistency comes in and makes it even harder. That is part of the role. The benefits? Parents and carers no know what they get from myself, and offer praise for that certainty, albeit it after the events. You should never lose sight of the end goal – to protect the learning environment.

> **My tips are:**
>
> - Create a folder for each student in your year group and file absolutely every email as this will help exponentially. If you have a conversation with a colleague, ask them to email it to you or write an email to yourself with the information down.
> - If it is an arranged meeting with a parent, ensure you have all information there, no matter how small it is, so you aren't exposed.
> - Ensure you know the school policies that are relevant to you – behaviour, attendance, safeguarding, etc.
> - Try and speak to parents or carers as soon as you can about issues, get your events in first before their child.
> - In meetings, try and be professional at all times – you set the tone for the meeting.
> - If a parent or carer becomes too much you are well within your right to call an end to the meeting and ask them to leave.
>
> Remember to be persistent, insistent and consistent and it is 'far better to have a fence at the top of a cliff than an ambulance waiting below'.

Questions to Ask of Yourself, Your Team, Your Staff, Your Students or Your Wider Community

Do all staff feel comfortable communicating with parents or external agencies?

Do we offer training, or guidance, to staff to ensure that communication home meets the standards we expect and achieves its purpose?

What methods of communication do make use of to engage with our community?

How often do we review the methods of communication we use and how often do consult with stakeholders on which methods they prefer?

How aware are we of data that tracks parental engagement and how often do we engage with this that is, website, app, parents evening attendance, etc.?

- Do we have staff who are experts, or frequently successful, in difficult or challenging conversations – do we capitalise on their expertise for training/guidance of other staff?
- How often do I/we reflect on conversations held with parents, or meetings in school, and whether there could have been opportunities for improvement?
- As pastoral staff are we are of particularly disengaged parents – do we have a strategy to try and increase their engagement with school?
- How regularly do we communicate achievements/successes with parents at an individual/group level? How often do teaching staff share successes in the classroom with parents and through which methods?
- Are we aware of the status of our school community and issues that may be affecting them outside of school – do we have systems/mechanisms for support in place where we know that there is a barrier to communication?
- Do we have an awareness of communication issues within our community – do we share documents, or key messages, in common additional languages?
- Do staff know how to escalate issues with difficult conversations or parents who are proving to be challenging? Do we have systems in place to support with this as a school/trust?
- Do we have a wider communications strategy which governs how and when we communicate with parents/carers?

 Pastoral Care and the Curriculum

The oft-repeated, difficult task of being pro-active rather than reactive in Pastoral Care is a mission that staff and leaders strive to achieve every day. We ask ourselves regularly how we can ensure that there is less firefighting in the role and in reality it's most often the case that we need to be better prepared. If we want to fight less fires, or at least smaller ones, then we need to ensure that we have all of the appropriate fire safety prevention in place – the fire extinguishers nearby; the sandbags to stop it progressing (not a reference to difficult staff, honest); the practises and procedures to ensure that we evacuate away appropriately and, on occasion, the giant helicopter to drop the contents of the Pacific Ocean atop your fiery inferno of pastoral problems. One of the most significant factors in doing this is ensuring pastoral care is a consistently woven thread throughout your curriculum – something I mentioned in earlier chapters.

It can often be hard to have the time to truly reflect upon where pastoral care sits within the curriculum if you are having to be reactive and it's a task that often stands incomplete in the face of mounting pressure. So, what can we do to try and ensure that our curriculum takes some of this pressure away?

In this chapter, I discuss pastoral care/behavioural expectations as a part of the school/trust curriculum and the power that explicitly framing, teaching and referencing your pastoral goals can have on the success of a school community.

The Intersection of Pastoral and Curriculum

First and foremost, you need to reflect upon the challenges that your pastoral teams; your community and students face – what are the challenges that permeate your context and that you see regularly arising either in or out of school? Bullying? Cyberbullying? Sexting? Mental Health/Wellbeing

Concerns? Friendship Issues? Whatever it may be that regularly takes up your time as a member of pastoral staff – where does it fit within your curriculum – have you ever thought about whether it does?

Pastoral Care is easily forgotten in curriculum conversations – here's an idea for you to potentially take forward. As a pastoral team, or pastoral leaders, perform the exercise above and outline all of the contextual issues you feel you deal with as a school that are dealt with by the pastoral team. The next time the school has a curriculum planning focus for faculties, divide your pastoral staff amongst them and have them each take along the list of items – ask faculty staff whether they might be able to fit conversations/learning material around any of the issues you face into their schemes of learning.

A great example is that E-Safety is a feature of the ICT curriculum and covered almost perpetually throughout a child's time in school – have you ever, as a pastoral leader, looked closely at what is taught and whether it meets the needs of your community? In the chapter on Safeguarding, I wrote about a child who had been sending inappropriate images of themselves to others – as a Computing teacher we took the opportunity to review our E-Safety content and adapted the material delivered to cover what was a clearly misunderstood issue within our community and ensure that we delivered the message, with sensitivity and care, to all of the students in Key Stage Three through their computing lessons.

The content has remained a feature since and when our IT staff inevitably discuss curriculum with inspectors or external visitors there is nothing more powerful than being able to share just how well adapted our curriculum is to our community's needs. We need to be able to have those conversations at a wider level though – who is to say that through the teaching of an element of History we couldn't reference and discuss bullying or in English address issues of confidence through public speaking explicitly linked to issues identified by pastoral staff. Too often, Pastoral Care and Teaching and Learning/Curriculum are seen as separate elements when, in reality, they exist to support each other.

Working on the Relationship Between Pastoral and Academic

This goes further into building strong relationships with Teaching and Learning and building your own knowledge of the curriculum delivered in your context – as a Computer Science teacher, I teach a tough subject that is difficult to pick up if you haven't started at the same time as everyone else. I would often criticise when a new student appeared on my register, because the group size is small, and it looks like there is space, as that's usually setting someone up to fail in a difficult subject. In lots of schools, this decision is made by the pastoral team during the admissions process. Now, a valid criticism is that it might be a failing on my part not to have flagged this up to pastoral staff but it's one example of how developing your own knowledge of the curriculum that's taught, for the students you work with, pays dividends in the future, and avoids that angst.

The great thing about the focus on curriculum in schools is that in most, there are now easily digestible curriculum mapping documents that, as a member of pastoral staff, you should be able to understand and utilise. A learning walk becomes more powerful if you know you are walking into History and that this week, they are studying Roman architecture, and that in the 2 weeks prior, they have been looking at Roman cities. This gives you the ability to see whether your students are engaging with the learning material that is being presented to them, and also gives you the ability to offer praise where you see positives. If you can marry the worlds of academic and pastoral support together and use your skills and experience to impact both, then you will be going a long way to improving the educational experiences of the students within your care.

Knowing the subject needs/curriculum for those you are responsible for also gives you opportunities outside of the classroom to open up conversations as well as giving you the opportunity to challenge issues. There is also the chance to share your knowledge of potential issues with teaching staff – if I know for example that in ICT a Year 8 with recent experience of sexting is about to cover this in an e-safety topic then I can flag this to the teacher and help them to tactfully deal with something that could have otherwise been an issue. If there are students with experience of domestic violence or self-harm, I might raise this with their PSHE teacher if the topic is to be covered.

All of these things are attempts to be pro-active and ultimately ensure that what could be a difficult experience for a child and will likely as a result land on your desk, is managed before it becomes an issue. Further to this, we can use our knowledge and understanding of the curriculum to develop the young people in our care – I spent much time with a young man with an interest in Astronomy in KS3 but for whom confidence and social interactions weren't strengths. I pitched to the Headteacher the idea of supporting him through a remote, GCSE Astronomy course for which I would shoulder all responsibility and the funding was given. This focus, on area of academic interest, opened doors for him to feel confident in himself and also feel that there was something about him that nobody else in the school was doing. It contributed to the development of a mature, assured and knowledgeable young man. If I reflect on whether I would have considered this pastoral work, or part of a pastoral curriculum, at the time I likely would not have realised that it was. This was an intervention to provide him with support – no different to assigning him a mentor or encouraging attendance at an extra-curricular club.

The work we do in Pastoral Care runs so deeply through the school and the more we realise the areas that it touches, the more we can develop it further and expand and grow the provision and support packages we offer.

All PSHE Education is Not Equal

Whilst mentioning PSHE it is important to acknowledge that PSHE programmes in schools are not created equally. For some, there is an expert department or individual in school providing the drive and vision to ensure that PSHE is an appropriate part of the school curriculum. In other school's it is a bolt-on and packages of lessons are bought in and delivered in smaller sessions or during tutor times. In the worst cases, PSHE is delivered via drop-down days expected to solve the ills of the world with one inspirational speaker and a reflection booklet. That sounds like a criticism, perhaps it is, but we must find ways to ensure that the children in our schools are appropriately educated about themselves and their health and experiences. PSHE must be an integral part of your curriculum, and student experience, in whatever format that may take or you will ultimately open yourself up to issues in school that would have been preventable or ill-prepared students who go out into the world and struggle due to their lack of knowledge.

You may not be able to hire a faculty responsible solely for PSHE or dedicate curriculum time to it each week but, if this is the case, then you need to consider that you may be putting your students at a disadvantage compared to others their age. If you can't do those things you must think about how the provision that you do offer can adapted to ensure that it provides that solid base for student development. This is also not me saying that there are not schools who dedicate great deals of time, staffing and funding to delivering PSHE and that don't achieve as much as others who do less – what is important, as I believe is being repeated often throughout this book, is that you regularly review and reflect to ensure that your communities needs are met.

This idea of a Pastoral Curriculum should be evident in every element of school life – your assembly calendar should be linked to key events, topics or milestones and re-enforce crucial messages delivered elsewhere. Trips, events and rewards can all be driven by a focus on what your community needs. Extra-curricular visits, clubs and activities all provide opportunities for young people that they may previously not have had – do you consider these to be elements of your pastoral provision? Are there any that you would say are specific to your pastoral provision? There are so many opportunities for Pastoral Care to permeate school life – how often do you give it the same focus as other areas of the school, which are so tightly planned and sequenced?

> **Case Study 11.1 PSHE: The Fire Marshal of the Pastoral Team**
>
> by Sophie McPhee
> PSHE Coordinator at a Secondary School in the West Midlands, Programme Director for the Change Your Mind Year 12 mental health and wellbeing volunteering programme, now in schools across England & Wales
>
> Pastoral staff often say that the job is like fire-fighting: once one flame is extinguished, another one pops up elsewhere, and it is a case of keeping these 'little fires everywhere' (to steal the title of the fantastic novel by Celeste Ng) under control. If these "fires" are the crisis moments in our pupils' lives – the person on Snapchat asking them for a nude selfie, the moment when a family argument turns into a DV incident – then it would make sense for us to give them some safety training in advance. If we visit a large building for a CPD course, they tell us what to do in case of an alarm; when we get on a plane, the cabin crew give us instructions for an emergency situation. What every successful pastoral team – the emergency service – needs, is to have their role supported by 'safety training' delivered to pupils as part of regular, timetabled, high-quality PSHE.
>
> It is not enough to run one drop-down day per year to 'tick the RSE box'. It is not enough to run some events for Mental Health Week and say, 'that's that covered'. It amazes me when I am told that a school doesn't really offer PSHE in any meaningful way on their curriculum, when it is the one subject we can say with 100% certainty that pupils will need later in life. Every single one of them will need to know how to look after their mental and physical health. Every single one will need to be able to manage their finances, conduct healthy relationships and contribute positively to the world around them as an active citizen. Every single one will be a consumer of the media. And let's face it, is there anything that can get us more inflamed at the moment than Twitter/X?
>
> When a Head of Year is finding that there are tensions within a particular form group, we can deliver a lesson on friendship. When a racial slur has been

> used, we can dig out our materials on hate crime and discrimination. Committed and passionate PSHE educators should be a mainstay in every school so that when a fire is burning, we can work to try and stop it spreading. An assembly on drugs, or safe sex, is insufficient – pupils need space to try out their voices, and have misconceptions addressed. After the Grenfell tragedy, we set about replacing combustible cladding – yet fires are raging in our pupils' lives every single day and not all schools are giving them the tools they need to look out for the first flame.
>
> A PSHE educator should not just be someone with additional time on their timetable that needs filling. They should be treated as a valued member of the pastoral team, an equal amongst their more front-line colleagues. It is in their lessons that the first faint whiff of smoke can come – the comment made about women 'asking for it', the casual mention of visiting incel forums – and so the quick referral to the Head of Year or Safeguarding Lead to take further action. So, to retain the analogy with which I started, good Personal, Social and Health Education is a complete approach to "fire" safety – smoke alarm, retardant and extinguisher. This is the equipment both our pupils and our fellow pastoral staff need so they are not fighting alone.

Bridging the Gap

Within the talk of a Pastoral Curriculum, it's also worth discussing how you build your cultural norms with students – expectations around behaviour, language and culture which can be taken for granted. Often, cultural norms are passed down via older students – the younger children see that they walk on the left because the older children are doing it – but how did the older children know? They were explicitly taught this. Behaviour, as a concept to be taught, is becoming more common within schools – bootcamps or transition events at the start of a year, which intend to train students in all of the essential behaviours expected of them at school. There is merit in these tactics in ensuring that the behaviours we expect within our schools don't, unless you are very lucky, just appear. We need to take every opportunity to teach and re-enforce expectations and folding this into the idea of our pastoral curriculum makes utmost sense.

How often do you take opportunities to refresh students on expectations of their behaviour or attitude in school – is this a re-active or pro-active measure? I have a clear memory of an assembly, whilst at school myself, in which the Year Group were told, in no uncertain terms, about how frustrated staff were by the poor lunchtime behaviour with regarding to queueing and entering/exiting the dining hall. I didn't remember ever being told how we were supposed to queue or enter/exit the dining hall. I was probably told at the start of the year. Could the school have avoided the problem arising in the future by introducing more times to refresh student understanding on these expectations or explain why they were so important? Definitely. It's worth thinking about how often you explain your school policies/rules within your Pastoral Curriculum – most children want to know why they are being told to do something and if they understand that 'we don't do ABC because XYZ' they are much less likely to do it.

Routines and expectations should be sacrosanct within your school and building in opportunities to discuss these, and practise them, within school time is essential – even if it feels like you are taking time away from subject curriculums – the knock-on effect of students who understand their place in the school is huge.

Case Study 11.2 Scholarly Behaviour Underpins Strong School Culture

by Chloe French
Head of School, Castle Mead Academy

Castle Mead Academy is a Free School in Leicester city centre, which opened in August 2019. We are a growing school, with currently year 7 and 8 pupils only. This period marks a critical phase in our growth, as we prepare to move to our permanent site and welcome a third-year group in August 2021. At Castle Mead, our tag line is 'Excellence in the heart of Leicester', and our diverse intake truly embodies the heart of our city.

At Castle Mead, we say that it is unequivocal that:

- Everyone is capable of excellence
- We develop the whole self
- We make no excuses
- Feedback is a gift

Every member of our school community subscribes to these four beliefs, and in turn they underpin everything that we do. This has helped us to establish a strong school culture rooted in mutual respect, self-efficacy, and high expectations in order to grow a community of excellence.

From a pupil perspective, these beliefs inform our practice in a number of ways. Words are important. Our pupils are referred to, and refer to themselves, as scholars. This word is empowering and loaded with ambition. Our scholars recognise that they are knowledgeable, learned young people. Staff and parents, in using this term, convey their unquestionably high expectations that everyone is capable of excellence. Excellence is about working hard, giving 100% and producing work that is "worthy of pride" (Berger, 2003), and our Teaching and Learning framework is geared towards supporting every single one of our scholars in achieving this.

The notion of 100% is paramount at Castle Mead. Inspired by Jo Facer in her book 'Simplicity Rules' (2019), our two ground rules are:

- Scholars focus 100% on learning
- Scholars follow instructions first time, every time

This level of simplicity allows for absolute clarity: all scholars and all staff understand exactly what these two ground rules look like in practice, and why they are so important. The 'why' is made explicitly clear, always. We talk to scholars about the importance of maximising learning time and showing respect. In addition, we talk to our scholars about the science of learning and how 100% focus is crucial in not overloading the working memory. This overcommunication of the 'why' ensures that we focus on purpose, not power. In practice, we support our scholars in meeting these ground rules through a series of carefully scripted routines, many of which are inspired by Doug Lemov's 'Teach Like a Champion' (2015) techniques (for instance, STAR and Threshold). We induct scholars into these routines when they first join us and provide regular opportunities for deliberate practice to promote internalisation. In the same way, staff also have weekly 'Expert Practice' sessions to develop confidence and expertise in implementing routines.

One of the most joyous things about working at Castle Mead is hearing the plethora of "Good mornings" and "Good afternoons" shared throughout the day. As part of our Castle Credo – Be Kind, Work Hard, Build your Character – we teach manners, and the value of manners, explicitly. Scholars are encouraged to always greet and thank staff and their peers. We promote the importance of friendliness and practise this deliberately so that our scholars feel confident in thanking their teacher after a lesson, warmly greeting members of their tutor group during registration, being gracious towards someone who has held the door open for them, and so on.

We provide rich opportunities for talk both within and beyond the classroom. We want our scholars to engage in powerful cognitive discourse, to formulate their ideas with clarity and to practise good habits for talk so that these

> become internalised. As part of this, we use the mantra 'Speak like a Scholar', and there is universal understanding as to what this means, and why it is valuable.
>
> A particularly powerful example of capitalising on the spoken word at Castle Mead is 'Poetry in Voice'. Our school poem is 'Invictus' by William Ernest Henley and, thanks to our Leader of Poetry in Voice, our entire school community can recite this (with vigour!). We do this at line-up, in tutor time, at the start of every assembly and sometimes spontaneously at social time. Scholars feel a deep connection to the poem's inspiring message, and every member of staff is empowered to reinforce this in their interactions with scholars. Our scholars are unified through their shared understanding of what is meant by scholarly behaviour. The collective sense of pride and belonging is palpable when we come together as a school, for line-ups or Poetry in Voice recitations. Ultimately, our scholars understand the value of hard work and personal responsibility, as this has been taught explicitly and continues to be unapologetically overcommunicated. This is never more evident than during the energising crescendo of an 'Invictus' recital, when the whole school community booms
> "I am the master of my fate:
> I am the captain of my soul."

The Whack-a-Mole Trap

Ultimately, the question at the start of this chapter was about whether we wish to be pro-active or re-active in Pastoral Care. I doubt there is anybody who can say they are solely pro-active in our ever-shifting roles but there are many of us who would say we are solely re-active. In order to truly get to the heart of this problem you need to reflect on where Pastoral Care sits within your school – is it a means to an end to solve problems as they arise or are you looking to develop within your students the ability to self-regulate and manage their own emotions and experiences?

If you suggest it is a means to an end, then I think you would be devaluing the colossal, exceptional work undertaken by pastoral staff in schools across the globe – and, in reality, I don't think anyone reading this would believe that. I would wager however, that many pastoral staff feel that this is the role they currently undertake – they are the child at the amusement park playing whack-a-mole – up pops a problem, hammer it down. We need to take charge of the development of pastoral care and ensure that nobody in our profession feels this way and develop a Pastoral Curriculum in our schools that each of us can be proud of.

Questions to Ask of Yourself, Your Team, Your Staff, Your Students or Your Wider Community

Is pastoral care a feature of your school's curriculum – do you have an explicitly stated pastoral curriculum?

Who is responsible for linking Pastoral Care into your school curriculum – is anyone?

Do staff in the school understand how pastoral care links to their faculty/curriculum areas? Do common pastoral/community issues feature within elements of their subject teaching?

Does your assembly calendar link to key events, messages and milestones within your school calendar and the wider world? Does the curriculum match this?

Do pastoral staff/leaders engage, or have the opportunity to engage, with faculty staff about content that may be troubling for students they are responsible for?

Do pastoral/safeguarding leaders/experts have the opportunity to influence areas of the curriculum that have wider impact i.e., e-safety?

Is PSHE explicitly taught within your school environment – is this regularly reviewed to ensure that the methodology allows for effective delivery?

Do your pastoral staff see themselves as pro-active or re-active – do they see themselves as exclusively one or the other? Do they understand their wider roles within curriculum development?

Do you offer opportunities for students to develop outside of the classroom which are linked to pastoral needs/achievements? Are these shared with pastoral staff as achievements/opportunities for support with specific students/groups?

How often do you communicate with students about cultural norms/expectations in your school community – do you explain why decisions are made?

Conclusion

As I write the final words in this book, I can't help but reflect upon the absolutely joyous moments that have arisen throughout my time in pastoral care – all the more acute as I have moved out of the field and into the world of Academic performance leading Teaching and Learning, Data and Outcomes. Pastoral Care has given me a unique insight into the lives of so many wonderful young people – I started my first pastoral role at the age of 19 and it's no exaggeration to say that it has shaped me both personally and professionally.

My views on supporting those most in need in our communities would no doubt be different had I not worked in some of the most deprived localities in my city/county. My belief in high expectations and aspirations for all derived from observing the stark, harsh realities of an environment where this was not the case and the young people's lives were altered forever as a result. The understanding that extra-curricular activity is the key to opening the door to many young people's futures. The knowledge that, ultimately, no matter what your role, you can positively impact the life of a child through consistency and care.

The world is an ever-changing place, and in order for us to keep up with it, as Pastoral Staff and school leaders, we need to ensure that the profession continues to develop and that we all reach outside of our own contexts and share our good practise and skills. At the time of writing this book Pastoral Care is still vastly under-represented when it comes to subject associations, CPD, writing, research and networking. If we want to ensure that pastoral care continues to move forward, against a landscape where budgets and external support are lower than needed, we must continue to be generous with our time and our resources. I hope that this book contributes to the increasing amount of respect and praise placed on individuals and schools who deliver absolutely exceptional pastoral care for the students we serve.

I have been privileged to work with so many young people who needed that little bit of extra support, time or effort to realise their potential. The months spent scouring vacancies and applying for apprenticeships after-school with a boy on the verge of permanent exclusion and the fear I felt driving him to his first interview; the student who spent much of his Year 11 on alternative provision and is now in the fire service; the Looked After student who is now absolutely smashing their time at university or the morning breakfasts spent chatting and repairing shoes or a blazer for a young man at the start of my career who most certainly sparked the realisation that this was a job where I could really, truly have an impact.

Whether you aspire to work in pastoral care; you already do or you are leaving it – thank you on behalf of every young person you've helped or are going to help. It's not always easy... in fact it's probably never easy but it is the most rewarding job in education and it's been an absolute pleasure to write about it.

I Leave You with One Final Salutary Tale from The Unique World of Pastoral Care

Sitting across the room from a very angry parent, who had brought his comically tiny guitar along to our meeting and informed me his main employment was as a jester for renaissance faires, the world of Pastoral Care couldn't be any more ridiculous. In our tiny meeting room, he proceeded to sing the motivational song he had prepared for his son – he wouldn't take no for an answer and I wasn't entirely sure what the appropriate response was. The situation had been further complicated by the fact I had cancelled the meeting around 3 hours earlier, a message the mother and student had received but the father hadn't. At this point, you will have likely realised that this very angry parent was singing his motivational song to an audience of one – me. How did I respond after this three-minute personal concert? A slow clap and an assurance that I thought the message was very good and that when his son did eventually hear it, I was sure it would definitely get the message across that he needed to stop disrupting lessons and knuckle down – in reality, I think his son might have curled up into a ball and died right there and then.. as I too felt like doing.

You never quite know where the world of Pastoral Care will take you, but one thing is for sure – there's nothing else quite like it!

Index

absence reporting 124
assembly calendar 12, 54
attendance 2, 4, 20, 30, 35–36, 60, 88, 90, 92, 94, 96, 98, 102, 118, 124, 130
attendance interventions 94
attendance leader 4, 30, 36, 102
attendance policy 20, 35, 88, 90, 92, 94, 98
attendance rewards 36, 96, 98
attendance support plan 20, 60

behaviour 2–4, 6, 12, 16, 20, 28, 30, 35–36, 46, 52, 54, 67–68, 70, 72, 78, 82, 84, 86, 102, 118, 120, 124, 130, 138, 140
behaviour expectations 30, 70, 84, 138
behaviour management 2–3, 36, 52, 67, 70, 82, 84, 102, 120
briefings 60

careers advisor 4
challenging behaviour 46, 68, 70
coaching model 52
communication 46, 54, 58, 67, 92, 112, 118, 122, 124, 126, 130
community cohesion 122
consistency 32, 54, 67–68, 70, 99, 142
contextual needs 6, 8, 67
counsellor 3–4
curriculum 2, 6, 20, 132, 134, 136, 138, 140
curriculum mapping 134

designated safeguarding lead 107–108, 116
detentions 20, 104
duke of Edinburgh 30

EAL 4, 36, 90, 126
e-safety 134
email communication 130
exclusions 16, 36
expectations 22, 30, 48, 66, 70, 84, 88, 132, 138, 142
external agencies 94, 98, 100, 102, 112, 114, 130
extra-curricular 12, 30, 34, 36, 136, 142

feedback 42, 100, 104, 124, 138

grooming 112

head of year 2, 4, 10, 26, 40, 42, 48, 56, 70, 72, 74, 78, 90, 128, 136
home visits 20, 114
house system 8

inclusion manager 4
individual needs 14, 30, 116, 126
interventions 16, 34, 94, 114

leadership 6, 18, 32, 34, 42, 51–52, 70, 122
leading assemblies 54
letters home 90, 92, 126
line management 36, 52, 102, 120

medical evidence 90, 98
mental health 3, 36, 58, 82, 114, 132, 136
mentor 3–4, 24, 30

non-teaching roles 4
nurture group 28, 114

on-call 4, 52, 78

parental engagement 130
pastoral curriculum 2, 6, 20, 132, 134, 136, 138, 140
pastoral integration 94
pastoral leader 4, 30, 34, 36, 38, 46, 52, 56, 58, 84, 102, 140
pastoral roles 1, 3–4, 8, 24, 26, 30, 35, 38, 48, 51, 99, 102, 140
pastoral systems 3, 6, 8, 36, 46, 70, 82, 88, 90, 98, 102, 104, 106, 108, 116
persistent absentee 92
phone calls home 122
police involvement 112
positive behaviour 16, 36, 86, 120
professional curiosity 114
PSHE 134, 136
punctuality 2, 36, 88, 90, 94

recording incidents 108
reflection 1, 10, 58, 84, 104, 124
relationships 20, 30, 44, 46, 56, 118, 124, 128, 136
reporting 102, 120, 124
reward systems 82, 98
RSE 136

safeguarding 2–4, 24, 35, 40, 58, 72, 107–108, 110, 112, 114, 116, 130
safeguarding officer 3–4, 72
sanctions 54, 76, 86, 94, 120, 128
school app 124, 130
school rules 60, 78, 138
SEND 6, 14, 36, 90, 92, 98–99, 102, 104

serious case reviews 108
sexting 132, 134
social services 3, 6, 68, 112, 114
staff development 6, 16, 26, 34, 56, 70, 134, 140
strategy meetings 104
student support 2, 8, 28, 30, 44, 46, 51–52, 54, 56, 58, 70, 74, 92, 98, 110, 114
student voice 8, 78, 82
supervision 110, 116
support staff 2, 4, 8, 16, 18, 20, 26, 30, 34–36, 44, 46, 51–52, 54, 56, 58, 60, 62, 64, 67, 70, 74, 88, 92, 98, 102, 106, 114, 122, 128, 134, 142
supporting staff 2, 30, 36, 48, 54, 56, 88, 134, 142
sweat the small stuff 68, 120
systems and roles 3, 8, 102

teaching values 2, 10
team meetings 20, 42, 60, 104, 130
termly attendance update 92
therapist 4
trust building 12, 14
tutor team 8, 36, 51, 54, 56, 60, 62, 64, 72

website 35, 44, 126, 130
wellbeing 3–4, 36, 58, 132, 136
wellbeing lead 4
working with parents 14, 24, 56, 110, 118, 120, 128

young carers 2, 58

zero tolerance 68

For Product Safety Concerns and Information please contact our EU
representative GPSR@taylorandfrancis.com
Taylor & Francis Verlag GmbH, Kaufingerstraße 24, 80331 München, Germany

www.ingramcontent.com/pod-product-compliance
Lightning Source LLC
Chambersburg PA
CBHW080912170426
43201CB00017B/2304